New Directions for
Child and Adolescent
Development

Lene Arnett Jensen
Reed W. Larson
EDITORS-IN-CHIEF

William Damon
FOUNDING EDITOR

Siblings as Agents of Socialization

Laurie Kramer
Katherine J. Conger
EDITORS

Number 126 • Winter 2009
Jossey-Bass
San Francisco

SIBLINGS AS AGENTS OF SOCIALIZATION
Laurie Kramer, Katherine J. Conger (eds.)
New Directions for Child and Adolescent Development, no. 126
Lene Arnett Jensen, Reed W. Larson, Editors-in-Chief

Microfilm copies of issues and articles are available in 16mm and 35mm, as well as microfiche in 105mm, through University Microfilms, Inc., 300 North Zeeb Road, Ann Arbor, Michigan 48106-1346.

ISSN 1520-3247   electronic ISSN 1534-8687

NEW DIRECTIONS FOR CHILD AND ADOLESCENT DEVELOPMENT is part of The Jossey-Bass Education Series and is published quarterly by Wiley Subscription Services, Inc., a Wiley company, at Jossey-Bass, 989 Market Street, San Francisco, California 94103-1741. Periodicals postage paid at San Francisco, California, and at additional mailing offices. Postmaster: Send address changes to New Directions for Child and Adolescent Development, Jossey-Bass, 989 Market Street, San Francisco, CA 94103-1741.

New Directions for Child and Adolescent Development is indexed in Cambridge Scientific Abstracts (CSA/CIG), CHID: Combined Health Information Database (NIH), Contents Pages in Education (T&F), Current Abstracts (EBSCO), Educational Research Abstracts Online (T&F), ERIC Database (Education Resources Information Center), Index Medicus/MEDLINE/PubMed (NLM), Linguistics & Language Behavior Abstracts (CSA/CIG), Psychological Abstracts/PsycINFO (APA), Social Services Abstracts (CSA/CIG), SocINDEX (EBSCO), and Sociological Abstracts (CSA/CIG).

SUBSCRIPTION rates: For the U.S., $85 for individuals and $299 for institutions. Please see ordering information page at end of journal.

EDITORIAL CORRESPONDENCE should be e-mailed to the editors-in-chief: Lene Arnett Jensen (ljensen@clarku.edu) and Reed W. Larson (larsonr@illinois.edu).

Jossey-Bass Web address: www.josseybass.com

Contents

Kramer, L., & Conger, K. J. (2009). What we learn from our sisters and brothers: For better or for worse. In L. Kramer & K. J. Conger (Eds.), *Siblings as agents of socialization*. *New Directions for Child and Adolescent Development, 126*, 1–12. San Francisco: Jossey-Bass.

1

What We Learn from Our Sisters and Brothers: For Better or for Worse

Laurie Kramer, Katherine J. Conger

Abstract

Siblings have considerable influence on one another's development throughout childhood, yet most human development research has neglected sibling socialization. Through this volume, we aim to enhance our understanding of how siblings play formative roles in one another's social and emotional development. We examine the mechanisms by which children are influenced by their brothers and sisters, clarify the ways in which these mechanisms of socialization are similar to and different from children's socialization experiences with parents, and consider the conditions under which sibling socialization results in positive versus negative consequences for individual development. © Wiley Periodicals, Inc.

This material is based on work supported by the Cooperative State Research, Education, and Extension Service, U.S. Department of Agriculture, under Project No. ILLU-793–357. Any opinions, findings, conclusions, or recommendations expressed here are those of the authors and do not necessarily reflect the view of the U.S. Department of Agriculture.

Siblings spend a great deal of time with one another—more than they spend with parents or peers (McHale & Crouter, 1996; Updegraff, McHale, Whiteman, Thayer, & Delgado, 2005)—giving them countless opportunities to learn from one another, examine their similarities and differences, and be influenced by each others' choices and behaviors. In addition to having ample access to one another, siblings share experiences that may have significant meaning and impact on their lives. No one else can fully appreciate (and perhaps commiserate about) the idiosyncrasies of their family life. They alone know what it was like to be raised by their parents and grandparents as their unique family history unfolded. In fact, siblings share experiences that no one else in their lives—not even their parents—may know about. Given these significant attributes, it is curious that so much of human development research neglects the investigation of sibling socialization in favor of an almost total focus on parental socialization. The objective of this volume is to address this gap and examine the ways in which siblings contribute uniquely to one another's social and emotional development.

A clearer understanding of how siblings function as agents of socialization will help answer critical societal questions, such as why some children pursue deviant pathways while others do not. A line of research begun with Patterson (1986) and pursued by Bank, Patterson, and Reid (1996), Conger and Rueter (1996), and others demonstrates that antisocial or risky behaviors in adolescence are related not only to parenting and family structure factors; siblings also have considerable influence. Growing up with a sibling who engages in delinquent behaviors could lead a child on a trajectory that may be quite different than had the sibling been a straitlaced honor student. The development of effective prevention and intervention strategies depends on an accurate understanding of the relative contributions of siblings and parents in shaping individual development.

Through this volume, we aim to enhance our understanding of how siblings play formative roles in one another's social and emotional development. We examine the mechanisms by which children are influenced by their brothers and sisters in order to clarify the ways in which these processes of socialization are similar to and different from children's socialization experiences with parents. Furthermore, we consider the conditions under which sibling socialization results in positive versus negative consequences for individual development. And as we address these issues, attention is devoted to contextual factors that moderate sibling influences, such as family structure, life course events, ethnicity and culture, gender, and demographic indicators.

Through the six chapters in this volume, we address the following fundamental questions:

• Do siblings indeed serve as agents of socialization for one another? How are these processes of socialization similar to and different from parental socialization?

NEW DIRECTIONS FOR CHILD AND ADOLESCENT DEVELOPMENT • DOI: 10.1002/cd

- What are the mechanisms by which this socialization occurs? To what extent are processes such as modeling, social comparison, deidentification, or the direct extension of support responsible for shaping sibling behaviors?
- What are the conditions under which processes of sibling socialization yield positive versus negative outcomes for individual development?
- How can we harness the positive aspects of sibling relationships to foster children's well-being?

In this introductory chapter, we evaluate the premise that experiences with siblings play formative roles for children's social and emotional development. We briefly review research that links sibling experiences with dimensions of individual and family development, and in so doing, we describe sibling socialization processes that range in adaptive qualities. In short, we contend that a host of social and developmental outcomes are likely shaped, at least in part, by factors that directly relate to growing up with a sister or brother.

What (and How) Do Siblings Learn from One Another?

Under what circumstances, and in what ways, do siblings socialize one another? The growing body of research on children's sibling relationships suggests several processes by which sibling socialization likely occurs. These processes can be described using the following incomplete and nonexhaustive set of categories:

- Observational learning and instruction
- Sibling interactions that promote the development of social understanding and socioemotional competencies
- Setting aspirations, identity formation, and deidentification in response to perceived sibling characteristics
- Shared sibling experiences that lead to unique forms of support and understanding
- Nonshared experiences that lead to individual differences and, perhaps, resentment

We briefly describe each of these processes in prelude to their deeper exploration in subsequent chapters. This discussion will set the stage for Tucker and Updegraff's analysis in Chapter Two of the relative contributions of sibling and parental socialization processes—the ways in which sibling socialization processes are similar to and different from parental socialization processes.

Observational Learning and Instruction. Perhaps the clearest form of sibling socialization is the formal and informal instruction that children provide to their sisters and brothers. Older siblings have been shown to be effective instructors in a variety of complex tasks, such as learning to tie a shoe or operate a camera (Stewart, 1983). Conceivably, elder siblings who are skilled in their style of instruction and their ability to scaffold learning in a developmentally appropriate manner can enable younger siblings to achieve developmental tasks at a relatively younger age. Whereas parents may be excellent teachers of expected behaviors in formal settings (at the dinner table, visiting relatives, going to a museum), elder siblings may be the best authority for learning how to succeed in the world of peers, particularly in contexts external to the home, such as school and the neighborhood (see Zukow-Goldring, 2002). Who better than a sibling can teach a child how to make friends, "act cool," handle insults and slights, open a locker, or rebuff a sexual advance? It is also the case that older siblings learn from their younger siblings—for example, as younger sibs bring unique talents and interests to the relationship.

Even without direct instruction, younger sibs regularly take notice of and often emulate their elder siblings' behaviors. Through both overt modeling and vicarious forms of social learning, younger siblings may become prematurely introduced to the social world of older children and adolescents, which may include learning undesirable as well as desirable behaviors. Rates of teen pregnancy and high-risk sexual behaviors, for example, are higher in families where an elder teen daughter has had a child (East, 1998). Sibling congruence in substance use (Rende, Slomkowski, Lloyd-Richardson, & Niaura, 2005), smoking (Forrester, Biglan, Severson, & Smolkowski, 2007; Harakeh, Engels, Vermulst, De Vries, & Scholte, 2007), and antisocial behaviors (Criss & Shaw, 2005; Williams, Conger, & Blozis, 2007) has also been reported.

Although modeling may be one mechanism underlying this type of sibling influence, it is likely not the only means of transmission. As discussed in Chapters Three and Four, the quality of the sibling relationship may be a critical moderating factor; sibling similarity in adolescent drug use and sexual activity is higher for siblings who share a close relationship (Rowe & Gulley, 1992). Following such a social contagion model, a younger sibling would be at higher risk of modeling an elder sibling's substance use if the pair had a warm relationship and shared mutual friends. Rende et al. (2005) tested this hypothesis using a genetically informed design that controlled for the genetic relatedness of siblings. They found that sibling contact and mutual friendships were a source of social contagion for smoking and drinking regardless of genetic relatedness. Thus, siblings' collusion (coalitions that promote deviance while undermining parental authority) and coparticipation in deviant activities during adolescence may be critical mechanisms of sibling socialization (Snyder, Bank, & Burraston, 2005).

Brody, Flor, Hollett-Wright, and McCoy (1998) point out that younger siblings do not necessarily observe their older siblings' substance use; rather, it may be that elder siblings' attitudes regarding the acceptability of substance use may be tacitly transmitted through sibling interaction (see also Ardelt &

Day, 2002). In line with this view, Pomery et al. (2005) found that substance use among African American adolescents was significantly predicted by elder siblings' earlier reports of their behavioral willingness to use substances, even when controlling for parental substance use, socioeconomic status, and neighborhood variables.

Drawing on research stimulated by Patterson (1986) and Bank et al. (1996), Slomkowski, Rende, Conger, Simons, and Conger (2001) highlight an additional process by which siblings may raise each other's risk for antisocial behavior: training in coercion that is learned and reinforced through repeated and escalating cycles of aversive behaviors performed by parents and children. Sibling conflict and imitation of siblings' antagonistic interactions with parents can also increase the likelihood of coercion among siblings (Snyder et al., 2005).

In summary, children observe and learn behaviors, skills, and attitudes from their siblings that may be quite different from what they learn from their parents. The processes that underlie these types of learning, as well as the circumstances and contexts under which this learning occurs during the course of normative and nonnormative family development, is explored in Chapters Three and Four, respectively.

Promoting Social Understanding and Socioemotional Competencies. Childhood sibling relationships are unique and important contexts for developing social understanding (Dunn, 1988). Linkages between early sibling relationships and later success in interpersonal relationships have been illuminated in several longitudinal studies. For example, Cui, Conger, Bryant, and Elder (2002) demonstrated that supportiveness to a sibling in early adolescence predicted support in children's friendships three years later. Sibling hostility was also predictive of later hostility toward a friend. Cui et al. noted that both sibling supportiveness and hostility are predicted by parenting behaviors; this is in line with their social-contextual perspective that posits that family interactional processes and parenting equip children (with various degrees of success) with social competencies that they can apply to relationships within and outside the family context.

The types of socioemotional competencies that are required of children for successful sibling interactions, especially in early childhood, are considered to be more sophisticated and complex than competencies required for successful interactions with parents (Kramer & Gottman, 1992). Parents invest a great deal of effort in establishing, maintaining, and repairing their relationships with children as they actively seek to understand their children's perspectives, accommodate to their needs and wishes (or provide a rationale for why they will not), and manage conflicts. However, as young children, siblings are less likely to perform these relational tasks and accommodate to one another's interests, needs, and desires. Thus, to achieve successful interaction with a sibling, children are challenged to communicate clearly, enlist persuasive and reasoning abilities, assume the perspective of another, and manage disagreements and conflicts in ways that may not be as essential with parents (Kramer, in press).

Of course the types of social understanding that are developed in the context of sibling interactions are not always prosocial in nature; social understanding may be demonstrated through interactions that may be perceived as annoying, irritating, or manipulative. Although aversive, these interpersonal processes may be quite sophisticated, reflecting not only a clear understanding of the sibling's unique sensitivities and vulnerabilities, but also skills in taking advantage of another's vulnerabilities to advance one's own position. For example, the ability to successfully cajole, dupe, irritate, or embarrass a sibling may indicate well-developed perspective-taking skills—skills that may not be demonstrated quite as well or as early in other social relationships. Even two year olds have been observed to use their unique knowledge to tease, annoy, or frustrate a sibling (Dunn, 1988). As Pernoff, Ruffman, and Leekam (1994, p. 1228) eloquently stated, "Theory of mind is contagious: you catch it from your sib." Chapters Three and Four provide greater detail about the ways in which sibling socialization processes may reflect or lead to advanced social understanding and socioemotional capabilities.

Setting Aspirations, Identity Formation, and Deidentification in Response to Perceived Sibling Characteristics. Older siblings set a high bar for younger sibs to reach. In a quest to be like their elder siblings, younger children may actually achieve more and at a faster rate than children without older siblings. However, the ability to emulate an elder sibling's achievements may be perceived by younger siblings as excessively challenging or, in some cases, unattainable. Whereas a climate of competition may be created in some families in which less skilled siblings are motivated to keep up with or even exceed their sibling's competencies in a given domain, in other families, less competent siblings may suspend these aspirations and channel their energy into areas distinct from their siblings' expertise.

Along with a shared history, intimate knowledge, and perhaps a desire to emulate one's siblings, research on sibling deidentification suggests that individuals are also motivated to carve out unique identities, which may be shaped in part by their perception of their siblings' attributes and qualities (Schachter, Shore, Feldman-Rotman, Marquis, & Campbell, 1976; Whiteman, McHale, & Crouter, 2007). As Whiteman, Becerra, and Killoren discuss in Chapter Three, children regularly appraise their own interests and competence in light of their perceptions of their siblings' abilities and accomplishment. The high levels of access and interaction typically experienced by siblings may lead individual children to strive to be different from one another in core areas. As Whiteman et al. (2007) describe, the research offers few clues as to the circumstances that lead sisters and brothers toward emulation versus competition. Although it is not yet clear whether processes of modeling or deidentification better explain sibling socialization, exploration of these processes should contribute to our understanding of similarities and individual differences among siblings.

Shared Experiences That Build Unique Forms of Support and Understanding. Sibling relationships can be important sources of support and validation for young children. Fifth- and sixth-grade children in Furman and Buhrmester's (1985) classic study reported that companionship (93 percent), admiration (81 percent), prosocial behaviors (77 percent), and affection (65 percent) were the most common positive qualities of their sibling relationships. However, negative qualities, such as antagonism (91 percent) and quarreling (79 percent), were also commonly reported, which is consistent with the view that sibling relationships are best described as ambivalent (Dunn, 1988), marked by fluctuating positive and negative relationship dynamics.

Growing up in the same family can facilitate a sense of solidarity that is difficult to achieve in other relationships. In many low-income families, and in cultures that emphasize familism (a value for cohesive family relationships; Updegraff et al., 2005), children may be regularly expected to care for younger siblings (Weisner & Gallimore, 1977; Zukow-Goldring, 2002). Early caregiving experiences may contribute to the development of sibling empathy, perspective taking, and caring (Stewart & Marvin, 1984). For example, Teti and Ablard (1989) found that many older siblings spontaneously soothe, comfort, and care for their infant siblings when distressed.

When parents face difficulties in their lives, children are aware of this. Sibling support may be especially important when parents are less available, as siblings often respond to parent unavailability by becoming "more responsible and nurturant" (Bryant & Crockenberg, 1980, p. 542). Sibling bonds have been shown to be helpful to young children coping with family transitions and stressors, such as parental divorce (Jenkins, 1992) or financial hardship (Conger, Conger, & Elder, 1994). With greater knowledge and maturity, older siblings may help younger siblings clarify their understanding of family stress and correct misunderstandings. Sibling affection may curtail the level of internalizing behavior problems faced by children experiencing significant stressful life events (Gass, Jenkins, & Dunn, 2007). However, negative life events and conditions may also create barriers to siblings' provision of support, or in cases such as foster care placement, to even maintain a relationship at all (Shlonsky, Bellamy, Elkins, & Ashare, 2005). Barriers and constraints to sibling socialization and support are discussed by Conger, Stocker, and McGuire in Chapter Four. Evidence presented in this chapter suggests that challenging life experiences may disrupt social processes between siblings; for example, when support from a sibling is not available during a time of stress or when sibling contributions are counterproductive, outcomes for individual children may be less favorable. Additional implications of sibling support for advancing children's well-being are explored by Stormshak, Bullock, and Falkenstein in Chapter Five.

Nonshared Experiences That Lead to Individual Differences and Perhaps Resentment. Although siblings certainly share a host of common experiences, we know that even when raised by the same parents, individual siblings may be treated quite differently, creating a nonshared environment for development (see McHale, Crouter, McGuire, & Updegraff, 1995; McGuire, 2002). In fact, even when parents treat siblings equally, individual children may have unique interpretations of these parental actions, perhaps due to differences in age, birth order, gender, personality, or other contextual factors. In this way, siblings may generate their own nonshared experiences, which may represent potent socializing influences on children's personal development.

Siblings have been described as vigilant in detecting instances in which they are treated differently by parents, consistently forming attributions about why they are treated differently (Kowal & Kramer, 1997) and appraising the fairness of these behaviors (Kowal, Kramer, Krull, & Crick, 2002; McHale, Updegraff, Jackson-Newsom, Tucker, & Crouter, 2000). Differential experiences that are judged to be unfair are linked with poorer sibling relationship quality, individual well-being, and parent-child relationships. In particular, children who report being unfavored are more likely to report depressive symptoms (Shanahan, McHale, Crouter, & Osgood, 2008), lower self-worth (Kowal et al., 2002; Shebloski, Conger, & Widaman, 2005), and greater externalizing and internalizing behavior problems (Conger & Conger, 1994; Kowal et al., 2002; McHale et al., 2000). Compounding these undesirable outcomes of parental differential treatment is the finding that siblings and parents report rarely discussing issues relating to differential treatment (Kowal, Krull, & Kramer, 2007), thereby limiting opportunities for children and parents to consider and correct unfair or insensitive treatment, and the resentment that may accompany such treatment. Chapters Three and Five address the ways in which nonshared experiences play a role in sibling socialization.

Sibling Socialization Outcomes for Individual Development. How can we take advantage of our growing understanding of sibling socialization processes to promote better outcomes for siblings? Stormshak, Bullock, and Falkenstein tackle this question in Chapter Five as they explore ways to harness sibling socialization processes that have been linked with positive outcomes while minimizing processes that foreshadow negative outcomes, in order to foster children's well-being. They advocate for an ecological approach to family intervention tailored to the needs of individual families while taking into account several key contextual and developmental factors. Their EcoFIT model (Dishion & Stormshak, 2007) explicitly supports appropriate forms of sibling interaction while strengthening parental management practices to improve the well-being of high-risk youth.

A greater understanding of sibling socialization processes will contribute to the development of prevention strategies that may help young siblings set their relationship off on a positive trajectory. Preventive intervention programs, such as More Fun with Sisters and Brothers (Kennedy & Kramer, 2008), intentionally build on socialization processes that promote the development of social understanding. Four- to eight-year-old siblings are taught a set of social and emotional competencies that have been identified in previous research as contributing to prosocial sibling relationship quality. Improvements in emotion regulation gained through the program have been linked with more frequent prosocial sibling interactions (Kennedy & Kramer, 2008). In addition, it appears that young children carry these prosocial skills into age-mate peer environments, such as child care settings, thereby enhancing opportunities for positive peer relationships.

As Stormshak, Bullock, and Falkenstein describe in Chapter Five, the promotion of successful sibling relationships and individual well-being is likely to be advanced through many of the key socialization processes outlined in this chapter.

Conclusion

Time magazine's Jeffrey Kluger (2006) contends that siblings are the people who "make you who you are" (p. 1). Sibling relationships are considered fundamental relationships that have an enduring impact on an individual's character and success in future relationships. Although the jury is still out as to whether sibling relationships are as potent as this statement contends— and if these relationships are more influential than other relationships that children have—it is fascinating to consider, as we do in this volume, the myriad ways that siblings may shape one another's development.

Potentially the longest relationships that an individual will have with any family member, sibling relationships offer countless opportunities for affecting each other's lives. Our ability to fully understand and harness sibling influences has critical implications not only for the development of effective prevention and intervention strategies that will promote successful sibling relationships but also has the potential to improve individual well-being across the life course.

References

Ardelt, M., & Day, L. (2002). Parents, siblings, and peers: Close social relationships and adolescent deviance. *Journal of Early Adolescence, 22,* 310–349.

Bank, L., Patterson, G. R., & Reid, J. B. (1996). Negative sibling interaction patterns as predictors of later adjustment processes in young male adolescents. In G. H. Brody (Ed.), *Sibling relationships: Their causes and consequences* (pp. 197–229). Norwood, NJ: Ablex.

Brody, G. H., Flor, D. L., Hollett-Wright, N., & McCoy, J. K. (1998). Children's development of alcohol use norms: Contributions of parent and sibling norms, children's temperaments, and parent-child discussions. *Journal of Family Psychology, 12,* 209–219.

Bryant, B., & Crockenberg, S. (1980). Correlates and dimensions of prosocial behavior: A study of female siblings with their mothers. *Child Development, 51,* 529–544.

Conger, K. J., & Conger, R. D. (1994). Differential parenting and change in sibling differences in delinquency. *Journal of Family Psychology, 8,* 287–302.

Conger, K. J., Conger, R. D., & Elder, G. H. (1994). Sibling relations during hard times. In R. D. Conger & G. H. Elder (Eds.), *Families in troubled times: Adapting to change in rural America* (pp. 235–252). New York: Aldine de Gruyter.

Conger, R. D., & Rueter, M. A. (1996). Siblings, parents and peers: A longitudinal study of social influence in adolescent risk for alcohol use and abuse. In G. H. Brody (Ed.), *Sibling relationships: Their causes and consequences* (pp. 1–30). Norwood, NJ: Ablex.

Criss, M. M., & Shaw, D. S. (2005). Sibling relationships as contexts for delinquency training in low income families. *Journal of Family Psychology, 19,* 592–600.

Cui, M., Conger, R. D., Bryant, C. M., & Elder, G. H. (2002). Parental behavior and the quality of adolescent friendships: A social contextual perspective. *Journal of Marriage and Family, 64,* 676–689.

Dishion, T. J., & Stormshak, E. A. (2007). *Intervening in children's lives: An ecological, family-centered approach to mental health care.* Washington, DC: APA Books.

Dunn, J. (1988). *The beginnings of social understanding.* Cambridge, MA: Harvard University Press.

East, P. L. (1998). Impact of adolescent childbearing on families and younger siblings: Effects that increase younger siblings' risk for early pregnancy. *Applied Developmental Science, 2,* 62–74.

Forrester, K., Biglan, A., Severson, H. H., & Smolkowski, K. (2007). Predictors of smoking onset over two years. *Nicotine and Tobacco Research, 9,* 1259–1267.

Furman, W., & Buhrmester, D. (1985). Children's perceptions of the qualities of their sibling relationships. *Child Development, 56,* 448–461.

Gass, K., Jenkins, J., & Dunn, J. (2007). Are sibling relationships protective? A longitudinal study. *Journal of Child Psychology and Psychiatry, 48,* 167–175.

Harakeh, Z., Engels, R.C.M.E., Vermulst, A. A., DeVries, H., & Scholte, R.H.J. (2007). The influence of best friend and siblings on adolescent smoking: A longitudinal study. *Psychology and Health, 22,* 269–289.

Jenkins, J. (1992). Sibling relationships in disharmonious homes: Potential difficulties and protective effects. In F. Boer & J. Dunn (Eds.), *Children's sibling relationships: Developmental and clinical issues* (pp. 125–138). Mahwah, NJ: Erlbaum.

Kennedy, D. E., & Kramer, L. (2008). Improving emotion regulation and sibling relationship quality: The More Fun with Sisters and Brothers Program. *Family Relations, 57,* 568–579.

Kluger, J. (2006, July 10). The new science of siblings. *Time,* 47–55.

Kowal, A., & Kramer, L. (1997). Children's understanding of parental differential treatment. *Child Development, 68,* 113–126.

Kowal, A., Kramer, L., Krull, J. L., & Crick, N. (2002). Children's perceptions of the fairness of parental preferential treatment and their socioemotional well-being. *Journal of Family Psychology, 16,* 297–306.

Kowal, A., Krull, J., & Kramer, L. (2007). Shared understanding of parental differential treatment in families. *Social Development, 15,* 276–295.

Kramer, L. (in press). Essential ingredients of successful sibling relationships. *Child Development Perspectives.*

Kramer, L., & Gottman, J. M. (1992). Becoming a sibling: "With a little help from my friends." *Developmental Psychology, 28,* 685–699.

McGuire, S. (2002). Nonshared environment research: What is it and where is it going? *Marriage and Family Review, 33,* 31–56.

McHale, S. M., & Crouter, A. C., (1996). The family contexts of children's sibling relationships. In G. Brody (Ed.), *Sibling relationships: Their causes and consequences* (pp. 173–195). Norwood, NJ: Ablex.

McHale, S. M., Crouter, A. C., McGuire, S. A., & Updegraff, K. A. (1995). Congruence between mothers' and fathers' differential treatment of siblings: Links with family relations and children's well-being. *Child Development, 66,* 116–128.

McHale, S. M., Updegraff, K. A., Jackson-Newsom, J., Tucker, C. J., & Crouter, A. C. (2000). When does parents' differential treatment have negative implications for siblings? *Social Development, 9,* 149–172.

Patterson, G. R. (1986). The contribution of siblings to training for fighting: A microsocial analysis. In J. Block, D. Olweus, & M. Radke-Yarrow (Eds.), *Development of antisocial and prosocial behavior* (pp. 235–261). Orlando, FL: Academic Press.

Pernoff, J., Ruffman, T., & Leekam, S. R. (1994). Theory of mind is contagious: You catch it from your sibs. *Child Development, 65,* 1228–1238.

Pomery, E. A., Gibbons, F. X., Gerrard, M., Cleveland, M. J., Brody, G. H., & Wills, T. A. (2005). Families and risk: Prospective analyses of familial and social influences on adolescence substance use. *Journal of Family Psychology, 19,* 560–570.

Rende, R., Slomkowski, C., Lloyd-Richardson, E., & Niaura, R. (2005). Sibling effects on substance use in adolescence: Social contagion and genetic relatedness. *Journal of Family Psychology, 19,* 611–618.

Rowe, D. C., & Gulley, B. L. (1992). Sibling effects on substance use and delinquency. *Criminology, 30,* 217–233.

Schachter, F. F., Shore, E., Feldman-Rotman, S., Marquis, R. E., & Campbell, S. (1976). Sibling deidentification. *Developmental Psychology, 12,* 418–427.

Shanahan, L., McHale, S. M., Crouter, A. C., & Osgood, D. W. (2008). Linkages between parents' differential treatment, youth depressive symptoms, and sibling relationships. *Journal of Marriage and Family, 70,* 480–494.

Shebloski, B., Conger, K. J., & Widaman, K. F. (2005). Reciprocal links among differential parenting, perceived partiality, and self-worth: A three-wave longitudinal study. *Journal of Family Psychology, 19,* 633–642.

Shlonsky, A., Bellamy, J., Elkins, J., & Ashare, C. J. (2005). The other kin: Setting the course for research, policy, and practice with siblings in foster care. *Children and Youth Services Review, 27,* 697–716.

Slomkowski, C., Rende, R., Conger, K., Simons, R., & Conger, R. (2001). Sisters, brothers, and delinquency: Evaluating social influence during early and middle adolescence. *Child Development, 72,* 271–283.

Snyder, J., Bank, L., & Burraston, B. (2005). The consequences of antisocial behavior in older male siblings for younger brothers and sisters. *Journal of Family Psychology, 19,* 643–653.

Stewart, R. (1983). Sibling interaction: The role of the older child as a teacher for the younger. *Merrill-Palmer Quarterly, 29,* 47–68.

Stewart, R., & Marvin, R. S. (1984). Sibling relations: The role of conceptual perspective-taking in the ontogeny of sibling caregiving. *Child Development, 55,* 1322–1332.

Stormshak, E., & Dishion, T. J. (2002). An ecological approach to clinical and counseling psychology. *Clinical Child and Family Psychology Review, 5,* 197–215.

Teti, D. M., & Ablard, K. E. (1989). Security of attachment and infant-sibling relationships: A laboratory study. *Child Development, 60,* 1519–1528.

Updegraff, K. A., McHale, S. M., Whiteman, S. D., Thayer, S. M., & Delgado, M. Y. (2005). Adolescent sibling relationships in Mexican American families: Exploring the role of familism. *Journal of Family Psychology, 19,* 512–522.

Weisner, T., & Gallimore, R. (1977). My brother's keeper: Child and sibling caretaking. *Current Anthropology, 18,* 169–190.

Whiteman, S. D., McHale, S. M., & Crouter, A. C. (2007). Explaining sibling similarities: Perceptions of sibling influences. *Journal of Youth and Adolescence, 36,* 963–972.

Williams, S. T., Conger, K. J., & Blozis, S. (2007). The development of interpersonal aggression during adolescence: The importance of parents, siblings, and family economics. *Child Development, 78,* 1526–1542.

Zukow-Goldring, P. (2002). Sibling caregiving. In M. H. Bornstein (Ed.), *Handbook of parenting: Vol. 3. Being and becoming a parent* (2nd ed., pp. 253–286). Mahwah, NJ: Erlbaum.

LAURIE KRAMER is professor of applied family studies in the Department of Human and Community Development at the University of Illinois, Urbana. E-mail: lfkramer@illinois.edu.

KATHERINE J. CONGER is associate professor of human development and family studies in the Department of Human and Community Development at the University of California, Davis. E-mail: kjconger@ucdavis.edu.

NEW DIRECTIONS FOR CHILD AND ADOLESCENT DEVELOPMENT • DOI: 10.1002/cd

2

The Relative Contributions of Parents and Siblings to Child and Adolescent Development

Corinna Jenkins Tucker, Kimberly Updegraff

Abstract

Guided by an ecological framework, we explore how siblings' and parents' roles, relationships, and activities are intertwined in everyday life, providing unique and combined contributions to development. In a departure from past research that emphasized the separate contributions of siblings and parents to individual development, we find that examining the conjoint or interactive effects of sibling and parent influences promises to extend our understanding of the role of family in children's and adolescents' social, emotional, and cognitive development. Understood within the context of family and sociocultural characteristics, siblings' unique roles as agents of socialization are illuminated. © Wiley Periodicals, Inc.

NEW DIRECTIONS FOR CHILD AND ADOLESCENT DEVELOPMENT, NO. 126, WINTER 2009 © WILEY PERIODICALS, INC.
PUBLISHED ONLINE IN WILEY INTERSCIENCE (WWW.INTERSCIENCE.WILEY.COM) • DOI: 10.1002/cd.254

Siblings and parents differ in the types of socialization experiences they provide for children and adolescents. Although they are members of the same family, children's and adolescents' roles, relationship experiences, and daily activities with siblings are distinct from those with parents. The examination of these daily encounters with siblings and parents promises to illuminate the unique contributions of sisters and brothers to individual development in early childhood. For example, consider the different learning opportunities offered to children when they engage in pretend play with their siblings as opposed to their parents. Whereas siblings typically approach pretend play as collaborative partners, parents frequently serve as observers and commentators (Youngblade & Dunn, 1995). Differential developmental impacts are likely to result from these two distinct social experiences even though they emerge from the same type of play.

A similar contrast may exist in adolescence as siblings share expertise about peers and romantic relationships that come from the firsthand knowledge of everyday life at school—a knowledge base that parents lack (Tucker, McHale, & Crouter, 2001). Again, the developmental impact of parents and peers on the social behaviors of adolescents is likely to be disparate. However, similarities do exist in children's daily interactions with parents and siblings that may be especially important for certain forms of development, for example, in learning how to negotiate complementary roles (for example, teacher-learner), develop complex interpersonal skills (for example, conflict management), and exchange support and companionship (for example, leisure activities). Thus, the nature and dynamics of children's and adolescents' relationships with both siblings and parents serve as a foundation for cognitive, social, and emotional development (Dunn, 1993).

This chapter contrasts children's and adolescents' relationships with their siblings to those with their parents. Grounded in an ecologically oriented framework, which highlights roles, interpersonal relationships, and daily activities as key building blocks of individual development (Bronfenbrenner, 1979), we compare sibling-child and parent-child relationships in terms of their role structure, relationship quality, and companionship and involvement (McHale, Kim, & Whiteman, 2006). Through this analysis, we aim to highlight the distinct roles of siblings in children's and adolescents' development. Recognizing that relationships with siblings and parents do not occur in isolation from one another but coexist (Cox & Paley, 1997; Parke, 2004), we further emphasize the significance of efforts to understand how experiences with siblings and parents, in combination, play out in children's and adolescents' daily lives. Finally, we consider the importance of continued exploration of how children's and adolescents' relationships with siblings and parents are shaped by sibling relationship features, such as age spacing and gender constellation, and characteristics of the larger family and sociocultural context.

Role Structure of Sibling-Child Versus Parent-Child Relationships

The unique combination of complementary and reciprocal roles in sibling relationships in childhood makes them distinct from parent-child relationships (Dunn, 1983). Complementary roles, similar to the roles described by Vygotsky (1978) that characterize the zone of proximal development, provide a variety of opportunities for a more experienced partner (a parent or older sibling) to guide the development of a less experienced partner. Complementary features can be seen when older siblings assume the role of teacher (Dunn, 1983; Zukow-Goldring, 2002) and younger siblings comply with older siblings' directions (Abramovitch, Corter, Pepler, & Stanhope, 1986) and view older siblings as experts (Vandell, Minnett, & Santrock, 1987). These opportunities are more frequent when the age spacing between siblings is wide (Youngblade & Dunn, 1995). Effective teaching, nurturing (Branje, van Lieshout, van Aken, & Haselager, 2004; Tucker, Barber, & Eccles, 2001; Updegraff, McHale, & Crouter, 2002), and the modeling of interpersonal relationship skills (Maynard, 2004; Tucker, Updegraff, McHale, & Crouter, 1999) are beneficial outcomes of complementary sibling roles.

Reciprocal role relations reflect the more balanced and mutual nature of child-child interactions (Dunn, 1983). Although uncommon in parent-child relationships, reciprocity of siblings' roles often is displayed by equal exchanges as seen in young children's conflict and shared play (Dunn, 1983; Howe & Recchia, 2005). Through these reciprocal interactions, children have opportunities for joint collaboration and the development of social competencies such as perspective taking and negotiation (Howe, Petrakos, Rinaldi, & Lefebvre, 2004; Howe & Recchia, 2005). Siblings' reciprocal interactions typically provide younger siblings with their first experiences in child-child interactions and offer important opportunities for skill development that may serve as a foundation for peer relationships (Dunn, 1993).

The developmental patterns of complementary and reciprocal roles from childhood to adolescence differ for parent-child versus sibling-child relationships. In childhood, complementary roles are characteristic of both parent-child and sibling relationships. During adolescence, parent-child relationships, though still retaining a clear hierarchical power structure, shift from parents being in the dominant position to guiding the child toward a more balanced relationship as offspring mature biologically, socially, and cognitively (Furman & Buhrmester, 1992). The nature of siblings' role structure also begins to change in adolescence when the relatively unequal status of older and younger siblings begins to lessen (Buhrmester, 1992), creating additional opportunities for reciprocal interactions, particularly for dyads who are close in age (Tucker, Barber, & Eccles, 1997) and sibling pairs who have close and supportive relationships (Dunn & Dale, 1984; Slomkowski, Rende, Conger, Simons, & Conger, 2001).

The distinct combination of complementary and reciprocal roles in sibling relationships offers adolescents types of support experiences that differ from those they have with parents (Seginer, 1998). Whereas the amount of support parents provide decreases with development (Buhrmester, 1992; Scholte, van Lieshout, & van Aken, 2001), siblings appear to be stable sources of support, even in adolescence when they spend less time together (Branje et al., 2004; Scholte et al., 2001; Tucker, McHale, et al., 2001a; Tucker & Winzeler, 2007).

Tucker, McHale, et al. (2001a) found that complementary roles in adolescent sibling relationships occurred when older siblings served as expert sources of advice about extrafamilial topics such as peers and dating norms. However, with regard to family matters, both older and younger siblings were viewed as equal (they had more reciprocal roles) in terms of their expertise, possibly reflecting the belief that siblings are more likely to understand and share similar views than are parents (Tucker, McHale, et al., 2001a). The nature and extent of sibling support vary due to family characteristics such as marital status (Dunn, Davies, O'Connor, & Sturgess, 2001; Tucker, Barber, et al., 2001b) and sibling characteristics. For example, siblings of the same gender who are close in age report receiving relatively more support than siblings of disparate gender and ages (Branje et al., 2004; Tucker, Barber, & Eccles, 1997). Recognition of the importance of siblings' multidimensional support roles for adolescent adjustment has led to increased inclusion of siblings in clinical and applied work (Gnaulati, 2002).

However, reciprocal support roles in adolescent sibling relationships are not always associated with healthy development. Some siblings actively engage in deviant activities together and encourage and support each other's involvement in such behaviors, being described as "partners in crime" and "co-conspirators" (Slomkowski et al., 2001). Such forms of sibling support are theorized as responsible for sibling similarity in deviance (Slomkowski, et al., 2001) and as related to higher rates of adolescent substance use and sexual risk taking (Conger, 2005; Rende, Slomkowski, Lloyd-Richardson, & Niaura, 2005).

The balance of complementary and reciprocal roles in sibling relationships, and their connection to individual development, may be shaped in part by the cultural niche within which the family operates (Maynard, 2004; Weisner, 1993). Complementary sibling roles are more common in non-Western (Zukow-Goldring, 2002) and Western ethnic minority cultures (Burton, 2007), most likely because of cultural traditions that rely on older siblings to provide care and socialization of younger siblings (Brody & Murry, 2001; Zukow-Goldring, 2002). In these cultures, sibling relationships, like parent-child relationships in Western cultures, are recognized as serving a primary role in children's lives. A clear distinction in older and younger siblings' relative status is retained across development. Thus, the significance of siblings in non-Western and Western ethnic minority families, relative to parents, may be as or more influential on children's and adolescents' development. For example, siblings may play a particularly important role in navigating school and community organizations in immigrant families where parents have little experience with the U.S. educational system.

The balance of complementary and reciprocal role qualities that characterizes sibling relationships in childhood and adolescence distinguishes this relationship from parent-child relationships. The combination of complementary and reciprocal roles, a reflection of individual siblings' diverging points of view and experience, coupled with an intimate familiarity characteristic of a peer relationship, provides children with unique opportunities to influence each other's development. However, the importance of complementary and reciprocal features of sibling relationships to development cannot be fully understood in isolation, but must be considered with respect to children's relationships with their parents and within the larger sociocultural context.

Emotional Qualities of Children's Relationships with Siblings Versus Parents

The intensity of siblings' emotional relationships makes them developmentally distinct (Dunn, 1983, 1993; Tucker, McHale, & Crouter, 2003a) from parent-child and other close relationships. Siblings experience a range and intensity of both positive (warmth, affection, humor) and negative emotions (hostility, rivalry) in their daily interactions. Sisters and brothers who frequently interact in positive ways (cooperation, shared fantasy) also may engage in high levels of negative interactions or conflicts (Dunn, 1993). Furthermore, there are substantial variations across sibling relationships in the intensity and frequency of positive and negative emotions (Dunn, 1993). For example, whereas some sibling relationships are characterized by high levels of positive emotions together with infrequent conflict and hostility, others are "affectively intense," with siblings reporting high levels of both closeness and hostility (McGuire, McHale, & Updegraff, 1996).

The recognition that positive and negative qualities of siblings' relationships are intricately connected in their everyday lives has led to exploration of multidimensional characterizations of sibling relationships. In contrast to research on parent-child relationships, which has commonly described different combinations of warmth/support and control/autonomy granting (Baumrind, 1991; Grolnick & Farkas, 2002), studies of sibling relationships have focused on the combination of positivity and negativity (McGuire et al., 1996; McHale, Whiteman, Kim, & Crouter, 2007). Studying preadolescent sibling relationships in European American families, McGuire et al. (1996) identified four types of sibling relationships that varied in the combination of positivity and hostility. Sibling relationships characterized by high levels of hostility and positivity were linked to relatively greater satisfaction in sibling and parent-child relationships as compared to relationships categorized as high in hostility and low in positivity.

NEW DIRECTIONS FOR CHILD AND ADOLESCENT DEVELOPMENT • DOI: 10.1002/cd

Extending this work to African American adolescent sibling relationships, McHale et al. (2007) found that siblings had primarily positive (high warmth and below average conflict and control), negative (low warmth and high conflict and control), or distant (low warmth, conflict, and control) relationships. In this family and cultural context, positive sibling relationships were associated with greater parent-child warmth and lower parent-child conflict for older siblings. Together these findings suggest that sibling negativity may have different developmental implications depending on whether it occurs in combination with high positive affect. Importantly, optimal patterns of sibling emotional quality may differ across family and cultural contexts.

The role that structural characteristics (gender constellation and age spacing) play in shaping the emotional quality of sibling relationships and developmental changes in these qualities may be distinct from that of parent-child relationships. Most notable, different emotional qualities are reported by siblings with different gender constellations. For example, European American sisters report greater warmth with their siblings than do brothers from middle childhood through late adolescence (Kim, McHale, Osgood, & Crouter, 2006). Along similar lines, over a six-month period when younger siblings were eight to fourteen months of age, older siblings increased prosocial behavior only toward their younger same-sex siblings (Dunn & Kendrick, 1982). Different patterns of change in warmth for same- versus opposite-sex sibling pairs also are apparent, with a U-shaped pattern of change for opposite-sex pairs and no significant changes in same-sex pairs' reports from nine to seventeen years of age (Kim et al., 2006). Consistent links have not been found, however, between sibling gender constellation and conflict/negativity, particularly in middle childhood and adolescence (Dunn, Slomkowski, Beardsall, & Rende, 1994; Kim et al., 2006).

Consideration of cultural norms across the globe sheds light on our understanding of sibling dynamics. Perspectives on the nature and implications of sibling conflict vary substantially across Western and non-Western cultures. In Western societies, sibling conflict is thought to arise from sibling rivalry (Mendelson, 1990), and parents often try to manage sibling conflict in an effort to reduce it (Kramer & Baron, 1995). In contrast, sibling conflict is not viewed as negatively in non-Western societies (Maynard, 2004). Non-Western parents often let siblings work out their conflicts without intervention (Zukow-Goldring, 2002). In addition, some non-Western cultures discourage conflict and take steps to promote cooperation between siblings (Beals & Eason, 1993). These different approaches to managing sibling conflict may mean that such conflict is differentially linked to developmental outcomes in Western versus non-Western cultural contexts. In summary, sibling relationships offer unique socialization experiences that arise from the distinct combinations of positive and negative daily interactions. Importantly, these sibling interactions, and the emotional qualities that accompany them, occur simultaneously with those of parent-child relationships. Therefore, investigating how the qualities of sibling relationships are embedded in the larger context of family relationships, particularly with respect to parent-child relationships, represents an important direction for future research that will extend our understanding of how siblings and parents contribute to children's social and emotional development.

Companionship and Involvement with Siblings Versus Parents

The amount of time children spend with their siblings and the nature of their shared activities (such as leisure activities and caring for younger siblings) provide opportunities for unique socialization experiences. In European American families in the United States, time-use data reveal that beginning in middle childhood, children spend more time with siblings than with mothers and fathers or with peers, teachers, or alone (McHale & Crouter, 1996). In adolescence, siblings continue to spend substantial amounts of time together in shared activities (Tucker, McHale, & Crouter, 2008; Updegraff, McHale, Whiteman, Thayer, & Delgado, 2005). Patterns of siblings' shared time may be more pronounced in cultures that emphasize familial interdependence, support, and obligations. In Mexican American families in the southwestern United States, for example, siblings spend an average of seventeen hours per week in shared activities—more time than they spend with parents or other extended family members (Updegraff et al., 2005). Cross-cultural research further highlights that siblings are frequent companions in a range of cultural settings (Weisner, 1993).

Insights about the developmental implications of the quantity of time children and adolescents spend with siblings and parents focus primarily on time spent with parents. There is evidence that higher levels of involvement with parents are associated with greater well-being for children and adolescents (Crosnoe & Trinitapoli, 2008; McHale, Crouter, & Tucker, 2001). The connections between quantity of time spent with siblings and individual well-being may depend in part on the activities siblings engage in when they spend time together (for example, caregiving, deviant behaviors, homework, leisure activities) as well as on the familial and sociocultural context in which siblings' activities occur.

Siblings' time spent in caregiving activities and the developmental implications of sibling caregiving has been a primary focus of research on the nature of siblings' shared activities. Sibling caregiving is more commonly undertaken by girls (McHale & Harris, 1992), particularly by the eldest girls in the family (Burton, 2007). Caregiving is more frequent for children, particularly girls, in family contexts that include a disabled child (McHale & Gamble, 1989; McHale & Harris, 1992). It is notable, however, that the amount of time siblings spent together did not differ in families with and without a special needs child, but the types of activities siblings engaged in did differ, with more time spent caregiving rather than performing chores.

Cross-cultural comparisons also highlight differences in sibling caregiving roles (Cicirelli, 1994; Weisner, 1993; Zukow-Goldring, 2002). In non-Western cultures and Western ethnic minority groups, sibling caregiving is a significant family responsibility that allows parents to provide for the family economically (Brody & Murry, 2001; Burton, 2007; Cicirelli, 1994; Maynard, 2004). In Western societies, sibling caregiving is more limited (Cicirelli, 1994) and most often occurs to provide parents with leisure time (Brody & Murry, 2001). Exploring the connections between sibling caregiving and children's social and emotional development in cultures that have differing norms regarding caregiving will provide insights about the developmental implications of caregiving across cultures.

The links between sibling caregiving and individual development are complex. In McHale and colleagues' work comparing individuals with developmentally disabled and nondisabled siblings, sibling caregiving was linked to children's anxiety but not to other indicators of psychosocial functioning, such as conduct problems, depression, and perceptions of self-worth. In addition, sibling caregiving was not a significant predictor of children's adjustment, although other family processes were, particularly mother-child negativity and parental differential treatment (McHale & Gamble, 1989; McHale & Harris, 1992). These findings underscore the need to understand the implications of sibling caregiving in combination with parent-child relationship processes across different family contexts.

Examination of the developmental implications of the quantity and quality of time siblings spend together and how activities with siblings and parents, in combination, contribute to child and adolescent development is an important future direction of research. Descriptive information about children's and adolescents' shared activities (watching TV, engaging in educational activities, sports) with parents or family members more generally ("family time") has been the focus of considerable research (Crosnoe & Trinitapoli, 2008; Larson, Richards, Sims, & Dworkin, 2001; Larson & Verma, 1999; McHale et al., 2001). Relatively few studies have explored the amount of time children and adolescents spend in different types of activities with siblings: chores, homework, watching TV, and sports, for example. Insights about similarities and differences in the frequency and types of activities siblings engage in, gained from comparisons of children growing up with typically and nontypically developing siblings, underscore the importance of considering contextual characteristics in future research in this area (McHale & Crouter, 1996).

Parents' and Siblings' Combined Influence on Child and Adolescent Development

Children's and adolescents' relationships with siblings and parents are intertwined in their everyday lives, providing unique and combined contributions to their development (Bank, Burraston, & Snyder, 2004). Until relatively recently, however, attention has focused on the separate contributions of siblings and parents to individual development during these two developmental periods. Examining the conjoint or interactive effects of sibling and parent influences extends our understanding of the role of family in children's and adolescents' social, emotional, and cognitive development (Melby, Conger, Fang, Wickrama, & Conger, 2008).

Person-oriented approaches, which highlight individual differences in patterns of development and the interdependence of family relationships (Magnusson, 1998), are integral to the study of how the influences of parents and siblings in combination contribute to children's and adolescents' development. The importance of different patterns or profiles across these two relationships for adjustment has been identified in cross-sectional work (McGuire et al., 1996; McHale et al., 2007; Scholte et al., 2001; Tucker, Barber, et al., 2001). For example, adolescents who are most confident about their future life plans report either a pattern of high support from both parents and siblings or a pattern of high support from parents and low support from siblings. However, adolescents who are less confident about future plans report a pattern of low support from both parents and siblings or a pattern of low support from parents but high support from siblings (Tucker, Barber, et al., 2001). Examining both sibling and parent support can shed light on which combinations of support are linked to more optimal future planning. Longitudinal findings provide stronger evidence of the advantages of considering the interactive roles of siblings and parents. Children are more likely to express behavior problems in adolescence (between twelve and sixteen years of age), when they experience both high levels of sibling conflict and a rejecting parent-child relationship, than when children experienced either one of these factors earlier in life (Bank et al., 2004; Garcia, Shaw, Winslow, & Yaggi, 2000).

Variability in how siblings and parents conjointly contribute to children's and adolescents' development is evident by comparing studies that focus on different domains of development. McHale, Updegraff, Helms-Erikson, and Crouter (2001) compared the role of parents and siblings in modeling sex-typed behaviors and found that parents were more influential than siblings on firstborns' sex-typed qualities but that firstborns were more influential than parents on second-borns' sex-typed qualities. Thus, gender role socialization, in the case of sex-typed personal qualities, may be characterized by a pattern in which children model the sex-typed attitudes and personal qualities of sequentially higher-status family members. By comparison, children's and adolescents' roles in parent-child and sibling relationships may differentially matter for peer relationship experiences. Parents' warm and sensitive guidance during play is linked to peer competence (Parke & O'Neil, 1997), but connections between complementary and reciprocal siblings' roles and peer experiences are more differentiated and complex, suggesting that simple carryover effects do not exist (Dunn, 1993). We next examine the factors that are important to consider when studying the joint contributions of sibling and parent-child relationships to children's development.

Parents' and Siblings' Contributions Are Shaped by Sibling, Familial, and Sociocultural Characteristics

Little is known about the conditions that influence the nature and extent of siblings' and parents' relative and combined contributions to child and adolescent development. Historically, research on siblings' influence on development (Koch, 1956) primarily focused on sibling status variables (such as sex of siblings, birth order, or age spacing); more recent investigations have included familial (for example, marital status, family relationship quality; Dunn et al., 2001) and sociocultural (for example, ethnicity; Updegraff et al., 2005) characteristics. Although the study of parent-child relationships has expanded to consider familial and sociocultural features, most of what is known about sibling and parental influences on development comes from studies on majority family forms (always married) and majority cultural groups (European Americans).

Exploring parents' and siblings' independent and conjoint influences in different family or cultural settings is an important area of research. The interactive role of sibling and parent support may differ, for example, in single-parent versus always-married families. Findings of compensatory patterns of support across sibling and parent relationships in disharmonious or economically disadvantaged homes highlight the insights gained from taking the larger family and sociocultural context into account. When parents in high-stress homes are distracted or unavailable, positive sibling relationships and the provision of support from elder siblings have protective effects for children and adolescents (Conger, Conger, & Elder, 1994; Jenkins, 1992).

Extrapolating from ecocultural theory, which suggests that cultural characteristics are primary in shaping the nature of sibling relationship experiences (Weisner, 1993), cultural settings likely also influence the nature and extent to which siblings and parents conjointly influence child and adolescent development. Cross-cultural comparisons of parents' and siblings' roles from childhood through young adulthood, for example, may show whether non-Western societies' reliance on sibling caregivers (Zukow-Goldring, 2002) continues beyond adolescence and is linked to social and emotional development in ways not evident in Western cultures. In sum, although sibling research historically has emphasized status variables when examining the independent effects of siblings on development, the inclusion of familial and sociocultural characteristics will illuminate variability in the combined effect of sibling and parent influence on child and adolescent development.

Conclusion

Children's and adolescents' socialization experiences with siblings and parents offer distinct opportunities that arise from involvement in family relationships that are structured in different ways. Recognizing that siblings' unique contributions to child and adolescent development are important and guided by an ecological framework, we highlight how siblings' and parents' roles, relationships, and activities are intertwined in everyday life. Further investigation of the interactive nature of parent and sibling influences will illuminate new insights into children's and adolescents' cognitive, social, and emotional development. We also recommend that such investigations continue to consider the sibling, familial, and sociocultural contextual influences. We conclude by proposing suggestions for future research that can further enhance our understanding of parents' and siblings' relative contributions to individual development.

One important direction for future research is the examination of how trajectories of parent and sibling relationship experiences are related over time and across development. Such data could help document the distinct support role siblings may play, for example, by serving as a transitional resource that fosters adolescents' autonomy from parents during adolescence. We could also learn how siblings' and parents' roles, relationship quality, and shared activities are influenced by shifts in extrafamilial social networks (for example, peers, romantic partners) in childhood, adolescence, and beyond. In childhood, high levels of involvement with parents and siblings may be linked to more positive well-being, whereas in adolescence and adulthood, strong ties to the family may compensate for (or reinforce) weak relationships with individuals outside the family. These different patterns of sibling and parent support may have vastly distinct implications for youth adjustment (Updegraff & Obeidallah, 1998).

Consistent with the findings of behavioral geneticists, parent-child and sibling experiences of individual children from the same family are not monolithic but may differ in important ways due to a variety of nonshared environmental influences, such as differential parental treatment, children's and adolescents' active involvement in shaping their own environments, and unique personal characteristics of individual children, such as their temperamental qualities or social skills. Future work should consider variation in the relative and combined influence of parents and siblings for different children in the same family. For example, because of their status as an only child for a period of time, firstborn children may experience greater parental than sibling influence as compared to later-born children in the same family.

Child and adolescent development may also be differentially affected by parental gender. The distinct interaction styles, activities, and roles of mothers versus fathers create unique contributions to children's development (Parke & Buriel, 1998), and these differences should be investigated relative to, and in combination with, siblings' influences. Within-family comparisons of mothers' and fathers' differential treatment of their two children demonstrate that fathers' interactions with their children are more sex typed than are mothers', particularly for opposite-sex sibling pairs (Tucker, McHale, & Crouter, 2003b). Sibling socialization processes may be quite different, for example, if children are raised by a single father as opposed to a single mother.

We highlight the importance of siblings' contributions to individual development for children and adolescents who have siblings. For only children, the absence of sibling contributions to development may be effectively compensated for by parent-child and friend interactions (Falbo, 1992). Such work is informative for the study of parents' contributions to the development of firstborns' versus those born later. An interesting future direction would be a comparison of how only children's versus firstborns' versus later-borns' parent-child experiences are linked to children's and adolescents' styles of interaction with peers, for example, in their expression of emotion or the nature of relationship roles. Such work would highlight the extent to which sibling experiences (those of negotiation or rivalry, for example), in combination with parenting processes, influence peer interactions.

The roles of parents and siblings often are examined as distinct influences on development, yet these relationship experiences cannot be separated in children's and adolescents' everyday lives. A greater understanding of how experiences with parents and siblings, uniquely and jointly, play a role in children's and adolescents' development and how these experiences are shaped by broader sibling, familial, and cultural contexts will provide a new perspective on theoretical and empirical work on family relationships and individual cognitive, social, and emotional development.

References

Abramovitch, R., Corter, C., Pepler, D. J., & Stanhope, L. (1986). Sibling and peer interaction: A final follow-up and a comparison. *Child Development, 57,* 217–229.

Bank, L., Burraston, B., & Snyder, J. (2004). Sibling conflict and ineffective parenting as predictors of adolescent boys' antisocial behavior and peer difficulties: Additive and interactional effects. *Journal of Research on Adolescence, 14,* 99–125.

Baumrind, D. (1991). The influence of parenting style on adolescent competence and substance use. *Journal of Early Adolescence, 11,* 56–95.

Beals, A. R., & Eason, M. A. (1993). Siblings in North America and South Asia. In C. W. Nuckolls (Ed.), *Siblings of South Asia: Brothers and sisters in cultural context* (pp. 71–101). New York: Guilford Press.

Branje, S. J. T., van Lieshout, C. F. M., van Aken, M. A. G., & Haselager, G. J. T. (2004). Perceived support in sibling relationships and adolescent adjustment. *Journal of Child Psychology and Psychiatry, 45,* 1385–1396.

Brody, G. H., & Murry, V. M. (2001). Sibling socialization of competence in rural, single-parent African American families. *Journal of Marriage and the Family, 63,* 996–1008.

Bronfenbrenner, U. (1979). *The ecology of human development: Experiments in nature and by design.* Cambridge, MA: Harvard University Press.

Buhrmester, D. (1992). The developmental courses of sibling and peer relationships. In F. Boer & J. Dunn (Eds.), *Children's sibling relationships: Developmental and clinical issues* (pp. 19–40). Hillsdale, NJ: Erlbaum.

Burton, L. (2007). Childhood adultification in economically disadvantaged families: A conceptual model. *Family Relations, 56,* 329–345.

Cicirelli, V. G. (1994). Sibling relationships in cross-cultural perspective. *Journal of Marriage and the Family, 56,* 7–20.

Conger, K. J., Conger, R. D., & Elder, G. H., Jr. (1994). Sibling relations during hard times. In R. D. Conger, G. H. Elder, Jr., F. O. Lorenz, R. L. Simons, & L. B. Whitbeck (Eds.), *Families in troubled times: Adapting to change in rural America* (pp. 235–252). Hawthorne, NY: Aldine de Gruyter.

Conger, R. D. (2005). Sibling effects on smoking in adolescence: Evidence for social influence from a genetically informative design: Comment on Slomkowski et al. 2005. *Addiction, 100,* 441–442.

Cox, M. J., & Paley, B. (1997). Families as systems. *Annual Review of Psychology, 48,* 243–267.

Crosnoe, R., & Trinitapoli, J. (2008). Shared family activities and the transition from childhood into adolescence. *Journal of Research on Adolescence, 18,* 23–48.

Dunn, J. (1983). Sibling relationships in early childhood. *Child Development, 54,* 787–811.

Dunn, J. (1993). *Young children's close relationships: Beyond attachment.* Thousand Oaks, CA: Sage.

Dunn, J., & Dale, N. (1984). I a Daddy: Two-year olds' collaboration in joint pretend with sibling and with mother. In I. Bretherton (Ed.), *Symbolic play: The development of social understanding* (pp. 131–158). Orlando, FL: Academic Press.

Dunn, J., Davies, L. C., O'Connor, T.G., & Sturgess, W. (2001). Family lives and friendships: The perspectives of children in step-, single-parent, and nonstep families. *Journal of Family Psychology, 15,* 272–287.

Dunn, J., & Kendrick, C. (1982). *Siblings: Love, envy, and understanding.* Cambridge, MA: Harvard University Press.

Dunn, J., Slomkowski, C., Beardsall, L., & Rende, R. (1994). Adjustment in middle childhood and early adolescence: Links with earlier and contemporary sibling relationships. *Journal of Child Psychology and Psychiatry, 35,* 491–504.

Falbo, T. (1992). Social norms and the one-child family: Clinical and policy implications. In F. Boer & J. Dunn (Eds.), *Children's sibling relationships: Developmental and clinical issues* (pp. 71–82). Hillsdale, NJ: Erlbaum.

Furman, W., & Buhrmester, D. (1992). Age and sex differences in perceptions of networks of social relationships. *Child Development, 63,* 103–115.

Garcia, M. M., Shaw, D. S., Winslow, E. B., & Yaggi, K. E. (2000). Destructive sibling conflict and the development of conduct problems in young boys. *Developmental Psychology, 36,* 44–53.

Gnaulati, E. (2002). Extending the uses of sibling therapy with children and adolescents. *Psychotherapy: Theory/Research/Practice/Training, 39,* 76–87.

Grolnick, W. S., & Farkas, M. (2002). Parenting and the development of children's self regulation. In M. H. Bornstein (Ed.) *Handbook of parenting: Vol. 5. Practical issues in parenting* (2nd ed., pp. 89–110). Mahwah, NJ: Erlbaum.

Howe, N., Petrakos, H., Rinaldi, C. M., & LeFebvre, R. (2004). "This is a bad dog, you know . . .": Constructing shared meaning during sibling pretend play. *Child Development, 76,* 783–794.

Howe, N., & Recchia, H. (2005). Playmates and teachers: Reciprocal and complementary interactions between siblings. *Journal of Family Psychology, 19,* 497–502.

Jenkins, J. (1992). Sibling relationships in disharmonious homes: Potential difficulties and protective effects. In F. Boer & J. Dunn (Eds.), *Children's sibling relationships: Developmental and clinical issues* (pp. 125–138). Hillsdale, NJ: Erlbaum.

Kim, J., McHale, S. M., Osgood, D. W., & Crouter, A. C. (2006). Longitudinal course and family correlates of sibling relationships from childhood through adolescence. *Child Development, 77,* 1746–1761.

Koch, H. L. (1956). Sissiness and tomboyishness in relation to sibling characteristics. *Journal of Genetic Psychology, 88,* 231–244.

Kramer, L., & Baron, L. A. (1995). Parental perceptions of children's sibling relationships. *Family Relations, 44,* 95–103.

Larson, R. W., Richards, M. H., Sims, B., & Dworkin, J. (2001). How urban African American young adolescents spend their time: Time budgets for location, activities, and companionship. *American Journal of Community Psychology, 29,* 565–595.

Larson, R. W., & Verma, S. (1999). How children and adolescents spend time across the world: Work, play, and developmental opportunities. *Psychological Bulletin, 125,* 701–736.

Magnusson, D. (1998). The logic and implications of a person-oriented approach. In R. Cairns, L. Bergman, & J. Kagan (Eds.), *Methods and models for studying the individual* (pp. 33–64). Thousand Oaks, CA: Sage.

Maynard, A. E. (2004). Sibling interactions. In U. P. Gielen & J. Roopnarine (Eds.), *Childhood and adolescence: Cross-cultural perspectives and applications* (pp. 229–252). Westport, CT: Praeger.

McGuire, S., McHale, S. M., & Updegraff, K. (1996). Children's perceptions of the sibling relationship in middle childhood: Connections within and between family relationships. *Personal Relationships, 3,* 229–239.

McHale, S. M., & Crouter, A. C. (1996). The family contexts of children's sibling relationships. In G.H. Brody (Ed.), *Sibling relationships: Their causes and their consequences* (pp. 173–195). Norwood, NJ: Ablex.

McHale, S. M., Crouter, A. C., & Tucker, C. J. (2001). Free-time activities in middle childhood: Links with adjustment in early adolescence. *Child Development, 72,* 1764–1778.

McHale, S. M., & Gamble, W. C. (1989). Sibling relationships of children with disabled and nondisabled brothers and sisters. *Developmental Psychology, 25,* 421–429.

McHale, S. M., & Harris, V. S. (1992). Children's experiences with disabled and nondisabled siblings: Links with personal adjustment and relationship evaluations. In F. Boer & J. Dunn (Eds.), *Children's sibling relationships: Developmental and clinical issues* (pp. 83–100). Hillsdale, NJ: Erlbaum.

McHale, S. M., Kim, J., & Whiteman, S. D. (2006). Sibling relationships in childhood and adolescence. In P. Noller & J. A. Feeney (Eds.), *Close relationships: Functions, forms and processes* (pp. 127–149). Hove, England: Psychology Press/Taylor & Francis.

McHale, S. M., Updegraff, K. U., Helms-Erikson, H., & Crouter, A. C. (2001). Sibling influences on gender development in middle childhood and early adolescence: A longitudinal study. *Developmental Psychology, 37,* 115–125.

McHale, S. M., Whiteman, S. D., Kim, J., & Crouter, A. C. (2007). Characteristics and correlates of sibling relationships in two-parent African American families. *Journal of Family Psychology, 21,* 227–235.

Melby, J. N., Conger, R. D., Fang, S., Wickrama, K.A.S., & Conger, K. J. (2008). Adolescent family experiences and educational attainment during early adulthood. *Developmental Psychology, 44,* 1519–1536.

Mendelson, M. J. (1990). *Becoming a brother: A child learns about life, family, and self.* Cambridge, MA: MIT Press.

Parke, R. D. (2004). Development in the family. *Annual Review of Psychology, 55,* 365–399.

Parke, R. D., & Buriel, R. (1998). Socialization in the family: Ethnic and ecological perspectives. In W. Damon (Ed.) & N. Eisenberg (Vol. Ed.), *Handbook of child psychology: Vol. 3. Social, emotional, and personality development* (3rd ed., pp. 463–552). Hoboken, NJ: Wiley.

Parke, R. D., & O'Neil, R. (1997). The influence of significant others on learning in relationships. In S. Duck (Ed.), *Handbook of personal relationships: Theory, research and interventions* (2nd ed., pp. 29–59) Hoboken, NJ: Wiley.

Rende, R., Slomkowski, C., Lloyd-Richardson, E., & Niaura, R. (2005). Sibling effects on substance use in adolescence: Social contagion and genetic relatedness. *Journal of Family Psychology, 19,* 611–618.

Scholte, R.H.J., van Lieshout, C.F.M., & van Aken, M.A.G. (2001). Perceived relational support in adolescence: Dimensions, configurations, and adolescent adjustment. *Journal of Research on Adolescence, 11,* 71–94.

Seginer, R. (1998). Adolescents' perceptions of relationships with older siblings in the context of other close relationships. *Journal of Research on Adolescence, 8,* 287–308.

Slomkowski, C., Rende, R., Conger, K. J., Simons, R. L., & Conger, R. D. (2001). Sisters, brothers, and delinquency: Evaluating social influence during early and middle adolescence. *Child Development, 72,* 271–283.

Tucker, C. J., Barber, B. L., & Eccles, J. (1997). Advice about life plans and personal problems in late adolescent sibling relationships. *Journal of Youth and Adolescence, 26,* 63–76.

Tucker, C. J., Barber, B. L., & Eccles, J. S. (2001). Advice about life plans from mothers, fathers, and siblings in always-married and divorced families during late adolescence. *Journal of Youth and Adolescence, 30,* 729–747.

Tucker, C. J., McHale, S. M., & Crouter, A. C. (2001). Conditions of sibling support in adolescence. *Journal of Family Psychology, 15,* 254–271.

Tucker, C. J., McHale, S. M., & Crouter, A. C. (2003a). Conflict resolution: Links with adolescents' family relationships and individual well-being. *Journal of Family Issues, 24,* 715–736.

Tucker, C. J., McHale, S. M., & Crouter, A. C. (2003b). Dimensions of mothers' and fathers' differential treatment of siblings: Links with adolescents' sex-typed personal qualities. *Family Relations, 52,* 82–89.

Tucker, C. J., McHale, S. M., & Crouter, A. C. (2008). Links between older and younger adolescent siblings' adjustment: The moderating role of shared activities. *International Journal of Behavioral Development, 32,* 152–160.

Tucker, C. J., Updegraff, K. A., McHale, S. M., & Crouter, A. C. (1999). Older siblings as socializers of younger siblings' empathy. *Journal of Early Adolescence, 19,* 176–198.

Tucker, C. J., & Winzeler, A. (2007). Adolescent siblings' daily discussions: Connections to perceived academic, athletic, and peer competency. *Journal of Research on Adolescence, 17,* 145–152.

Updegraff, K. A., McHale, S. M., & Crouter, A. C. (2002). Adolescents' sibling relationship and friendship experiences: Developmental patterns and relationship linkages. *Social Development, 11,* 182–204.

Updegraff, K. A., McHale, S. M., Whiteman, S. D., Thayer, S. M., & Delgado, M. Y. (2005). Adolescent sibling relationships in Mexican American families: Exploring the role of familism. *Journal of Family Psychology, 19,* 512–522.

Updegraff, K. A., & Obeidallah, D. A. (1998). Young adolescents' patterns of involvement with siblings and friends. *Social Development, 8,* 52–69.

Vandell, D. L., Minnett, A. M., & Santrock, J. W. (1987). Age differences in sibling relationships during middle childhood. *Journal of Applied Developmental Psychology, 8,* 247–257.

Vygotsky, L. S. (1978). *Mind in society: The development of higher psychological processes.* Cambridge, MA: Harvard University Press.

Weisner, T. S. (1993). Ethnographic and ecocultural perspectives on sibling relationships. In Z. Stoneman & P. W. Berman (Eds.), *The effects of mental retardation, disability, and illness on sibling relationships: Research issues and challenges* (pp. 51–83). Baltimore, MD: Paul H. Brookes Publishing.

Youngblade, L. M., & Dunn, J. (1995). Individual differences in young children's pretend play with mother and sibling: Links to relationships and understanding of other people's feelings and beliefs. *Child Development, 66,* 1472–1492.

Zukow-Goldring, P. (2002). Sibling caregiving. In M. H. Bornstein (Ed.), *Handbook of parenting: Vol. 3. Being and becoming a parent* (2nd ed., pp. 253–286). Mahwah, NJ: Erlbaum.

CORINNA JENKINS TUCKER is an associate professor of family studies, Department of Family Studies, University of New Hampshire, Durham. E-mail: cjtucker@unh.edu.

KIMBERLY UPDEGRAFF is the Cowden Distinguished Professor of Family and Human Development, School of Social and Family Dynamics, Arizona State University, Tempe. E-mail: kimberly.updegraff@asu.edu.

Whiteman, S. D., Becerra, J. M., & Killoren, S. E. (2009). Mechanisms of sibling socialization in normative family development. In L. Kramer & K. J. Conger (Eds.), *Siblings as
agents of socialization. New Directions for Child and Adolescent Development*, 126, 29–43.
San Francisco: Jossey-Bass.

3

Mechanisms of Sibling Socialization in Normative Family Development

Shawn D. Whiteman, Julia M. Becerra, Sarah E. Killoren

Abstract

*Siblings are important sources of social influence throughout childhood and ado-
lescence. Nevertheless, the processes by which siblings influence one another
remain relatively unexplored. We highlight two theories of sibling influence—
sibling deidentification and social learning—that offer insights as to how and
why siblings develop similar and different attributes, attitudes, and behaviors.
Recognizing the need to move past post hoc explanations, we suggest several
directions for how these two influence processes can be measured directly in
future work. Research on sibling influence also can be improved by integrating
these theories and attending to their domains of influence. © Wiley Periodicals, Inc.*

New Directions for Child and Adolescent Development, no. 126, Winter 2009 © Wiley Periodicals, Inc.
Published online in Wiley InterScience (www.interscience.wiley.com) • DOI: 10.1002/cd.255

In recent years, developmental and family scholars have become increasingly interested in how siblings influence one another. Because of the amount of time they spend together and the emotional intensity of the relationship, researchers have pointed to the sibling relationship as an important context for social and cognitive development (for a review, see Brody, 1998). Consistent with this notion, a body of work indicates that children and youth develop important skills and capabilities through their direct interactions with their siblings, such as conflict resolution, perspective taking, negotiation, compromising, cooperation, and other forms of social competence (Brody & Murry, 2001; Dunn, Brown, Slomkowski, Tesla, & Youngblade, 1991; Katz, Kramer, & Gottman, 1992).

In addition to influencing each other through their everyday actions, research and theory on sibling influence highlight two opposing socialization processes—sibling deidentification, which operates to make siblings different, and social learning, which operates to make siblings alike—that help explain why some siblings are more alike and others more different in their attributes. Although these two theories are not alone in explaining why sibling similarities (shared genetics and shared environments, including shared parenting) and differences (nonshared genetics and nonshared environments, including parents' differential treatment) may develop, they have been invoked as explanations across a wide range of studies. Given their prominence in the literature, as well as their potential for future application, we review both theoretical and empirical research that supports sibling deidentification and social learning processes as explanations for sibling differences and similarities and highlight new directions for future research on sibling influence.

Sibling Deidentification and Sibling Differences

Research in the field of behavioral genetics reveals that in the areas of personality, intelligence, and well-being, siblings tend to be no more similar to one another than unrelated youth (Dunn & Plomin, 1990; Plomin & Daniels, 1987). Although the literature on behavioral genetics suggests that differences between siblings are the result of nonshared genes and nonshared environments, differences also occur because of a sibling relationship dynamic termed *sibling deidentification*. Sibling deidentification refers to the tendency for siblings to consciously or unconsciously select different niches and develop different personal qualities in order to define themselves as unique or dissimilar from one another.

Theorists have offered many explanations for sibling deidentification. Although these explanations are theoretically and conceptually distinct, most center on the idea that deidentification dynamics help protect siblings from social comparison, rivalry, envy, and possible resentment (Feinberg & Hetherington, 2000; Festinger, 1954; Schachter, Shore, Feldman-Rotman, Marquis, & Campbell 1976; Tesser, 1980; see also Sulloway, 1996). For example, if an older sibling excels at basketball, deidentification theories predict that the younger sibling will consciously or unconsciously choose to specialize in a different domain, such as art, or a different sport, such as soccer. Toward the end of reducing competition and rivalry, sibling deidentification processes are posited to operate more strongly when siblings are more objectively similar, such as when they are close in age and of the same sex (Schachter et al., 1976; Schachter, Gilutz, Shore, & Adler, 1978).

Psychodynamic theories suggest that identifying with or imitating siblings serves to exacerbate sibling rivalry as siblings seek the same goals, achievements, and gratifications. From this perspective, sibling deidentification is a defense mechanism that mitigates sibling competition and rivalry (Schachter et al., 1976). Consequently, sibling deidentification is posited to promote more positive relationships between siblings, marked by less conflict and greater warmth.

Social comparison theory (Feinberg, Neiderhiser, Simmens, Reiss, & Hetherington, 2000; Festinger, 1954) also predicts that siblings actively work to define themselves as different in order to reduce the costs of rivalry, competition, and comparison, albeit for different reasons. Social comparison theory emphasizes that one way in which individuals learn about themselves is through comparison with others. Such social comparison between siblings will likely demonstrate that one sibling is superior, thereby breeding resentment, envy, and possibly reduced self-esteem (Festinger, 1954). To avoid such negative consequences to the self, deidentification occurs as siblings direct themselves to different objectives, activities, and social circles.

Similarly, in applying self-esteem maintenance dynamics to the study of sibling relationships, Tesser (1980) suggested that siblings differentiate in order to maintain self-esteem. Tesser offered a more nuanced perspective on social comparison by suggesting that siblings will deidentify in domains that are highly relevant to each person's self-definition, such that they can avoid being compared on characteristics that they hold high in regard. Thus, self-esteem maintenance theory posits that sibling deidentification acts as a defense against the possible loss of self-esteem by reducing social comparison and rivalry on traits and characteristics important to self-definition. Importantly, Tesser's theory allows the possibility of similarities between siblings in domains that are not deemed as essential to their self-definition.

Despite theoretical insight as to why sibling deidentification dynamics operates within families, little empirical research has been conducted to explore this dynamic. In fact, much of the literature on sibling deidentification has been conducted by only one group of researchers, spearheaded by the late Frances Fuchs Schachter. Initially, Schachter et al. (1976) examined sibling deidentification in a sample of 383 college students and then replicated their findings with a sample of 140 mothers (Schachter et al., 1978). Across these two studies, Schachter and colleagues found three consistent patterns. First, in analyzing respondents' reports of whether siblings were alike or different, Schachter et al. (1976) found that sibling differentiation

NEW DIRECTIONS FOR CHILD AND ADOLESCENT DEVELOPMENT • DOI: 10.1002/cd

(which they equated with deidentification) occurred at its highest levels between first- and second-born offspring. Siblings in these dyads were rated as being different about twice as often as they were rated as being similar. Second, pairs of siblings (for example, second- and third-born siblings) were rated as being different at intermediate levels, with the smallest differences found for jump pairs of siblings (say, first- and third-born siblings). In both consecutive pairs of siblings, rates of deidentification were significantly higher than for the jump pairs, suggesting that birth order may moderate rates of sibling deidentification. Third, in analyzing personality ratings of the siblings, Schachter et al. found that sibling dyads who were rated as being different also were more polarized (one sibling happy and the other sad, for example) on a greater number of characteristics than were siblings who were rated as alike. Finally, deidentification was found to be greatest in same-sex sibling pairs as compared to opposite-sex sibling pairs.

In addition to these early studies, Schachter and Stone (1985) assessed the relation between sibling deidentification dynamics and temperament. In this study, 204 mothers were asked to contrast their young children in terms of their global temperaments. Similar to earlier findings (Schachter et al., 1976, 1978), differentiation was greatest for first- and second-born siblings. There also was limited evidence that deidentification was greater for same-sex siblings.

Developmental and family scholars have obtained support for the operation of sibling deidentification dynamics in the areas of vocational interests, gender role orientation, and adjustment. With respect to vocational interests, Grotevant (1978) found that adolescent girls with sisters reported fewer feminine interests than did girls with brothers. Similarly, in a sample of college-aged males, Leventhal (1970) discovered that second-borns reported more "masculine" vocational and activity interests (for example, engineering, outdoor, and technical interests) when they had older sisters as compared to those with brothers. In studying siblings' gender role orientations over a two-year period, McHale, Updegraff, Helms-Erikson, and Crouter (2001) observed that first-born, adolescent-age siblings became more different from their younger siblings over time. Finally, consistent with the notion that deidentification dynamics are more prevalent for siblings who are more similar, Feinberg and Hetherington (2000) found in a nationally representative sample that in general, siblings closer in age were less similar (or more different) across a range of personal adjustment indices than siblings further apart in age.

New Approaches for Studying Sibling Deidentification

Taken together, this small group of studies suggests that sibling deidentification dynamics may operate to make siblings different from one another. Unfortunately, these studies fail to measure these processes directly. Instead, deidentification dynamics are posited as post hoc explanations for patterns of differences between siblings. Future research needs to address this limitation by measuring influence processes more directly. For example, a series of recent studies by Whiteman and colleagues (Whiteman & Christiansen, 2008; Whiteman, McHale, & Crouter, 2007a; 2007b) demonstrated that sibling differentiation processes can be measured in a variety of ways.

First, using a qualitative approach, Whiteman and Christiansen (2008) asked first- and second-born siblings from 192 families to respond to open-ended questions about how their brothers and sisters influenced them. They found that 40 percent of second-borns and 31 percent of firstborns reported trying to differentiate from their brothers or sisters in some way. For example, one youth said, "I try to be as much different than her as I can because she doesn't try hard at anything and I don't want to be like that," and another said, "Are we allowed to talk about drugs and alcohol? [He] got into a lot of trouble and was grounded doing certain things, and like I never really had a desire to do any of it, like I learned not to do it" (p. 28).

Second, Whiteman and colleagues (2007a) asked second-born siblings to indicate on Likert scales the extent to which they tried to be like, be different from, and competed with their older siblings in four domains: athletics, arts, academics, and conduct. Adopting a person-oriented approach, Whiteman et al. discovered that 27 percent of second-borns' reports of sibling influence were characterized by differentiation dynamics, with these children reporting high levels of trying to be different from their elder sibling, low levels of trying to be like, and low levels of competition across all four domains. Furthermore, these differentiation dynamics were related to patterns of dissimilarity between siblings' activities and behaviors. Inconsistent with deidentification theory and earlier research, Whiteman and colleagues did not detect any associations between differentiation dynamics and the sex composition of the sibling dyad.

Although these recent reports show that sibling influence processes can be measured, future research must measure these phenomena in creative ways because deidentification dynamics are thought to occur both consciously and unconsciously. Qualitative approaches to studying sibling influences offer an important direction for future work as they enable researchers to capture subtle and nuanced patterns of sibling influence. For example, reports that systematically mention brothers' or sisters' activities and abilities as reasons that a child chooses certain behaviors or exhibits certain qualities may be evidence that siblings' personal qualities and characteristics are influential to youth's self-definitions. Experimental designs can also be used to test the theoretical underpinnings of deidentification theory. For example, Tesser's (1980) self-esteem maintenance theory provides a set of testable assumptions regarding when and under which contexts differentiation should occur. By manipulating those assumptions (for example, outcome relevance, sibling performance), researchers may discover the pervasiveness and conditions under which deidentification dynamics operate.

NEW DIRECTIONS FOR CHILD AND ADOLESCENT DEVELOPMENT • DOI: 10.1002/cd

Because much of the early work on sibling deidentification was limited to one respondent per family, future inquiry should also broaden designs to include multiple siblings per family. For example, using a design that included first- and second-born siblings, Whiteman and Christiansen (2008) found that differentiation dynamics were relevant for older as well as younger siblings, suggesting that siblings mutually view each other as having distinct characteristics and behaviors. This finding is notable because it challenges traditional deidentification assumptions that younger siblings differentiate from their older brothers and sisters, but not vice versa. Therefore, it is important that future research include the perspectives of multiple siblings, especially in large family systems, so that hypotheses about reciprocal influences, as well as the contributions of birth order and sex constellation, can be tested.

The literature on sibling deidentification is also limited because it has mainly focused on a narrow range of personality and temperament characteristics. Although siblings may exhibit different personality characteristics in order to show uniqueness and carve out their own niches within their shared environments, it is likely that deidentification dynamics operate in other domains as well. For example, as we review in the next section, the literature on sibling similarities reveals that older and younger siblings show modest similarity in their attitudes and behaviors regarding substance use, sexuality, aggressive and delinquent behaviors. Largely absent from this literature is attention as to how processes of differentiation may also operate to make siblings different with respect to risky and deviant behaviors. Thus, another direction for future research is to examine whether siblings deidentify across a wide range of domains, including their attitudes, behaviors, and competencies.

It is also possible that due to variations in children's personal definitions, preferences, and objectives, deidentification dynamics may operate in one domain of development (say, personality) and not in others (interest in sports). Consistent with Tesser's self-esteem maintenance theory, the extent to which certain characteristics and personal qualities are central to an individual's self-definition may influence whether deidentification dynamics emerge. For example, if a younger sibling places emphasis on his or her prowess in athletics, deidentification theory predicts that this child would choose to participate in sports in which the older sibling does not excel in, thereby avoiding downward social comparison. If, however, athletic competence is not central to either an older or a younger sibling's self-definition, then similarity in athletic interests and activities may not have meaningful implications. Unfortunately, the centrality of deidentification dynamics in the lives of siblings cannot be ascertained from current research. As a result, future research should examine deidentification dynamics across a range of characteristics and behaviors and also explore the correlates of those dynamics (for example, competence in domains, personal salience). Furthermore, given that

NEW DIRECTIONS FOR CHILD AND ADOLESCENT DEVELOPMENT • DOI: 10.1002/cd

sibling relationships are situated within larger family contexts, it is important to attend to socialization (for example, the importance placed on specific domains), values imparted by parents, and the broader cultural context.

Future research should also link deidentification processes to qualities of the sibling relationship. Although deidentification theories make predictions that differentiation should be related to less sibling conflict and rivalry, only a few studies have examined these associations. Supporting the idea that differentiation works to reduce sibling rivalry, Feinberg, McHale, Crouter, and Cumsille (2003) showed that siblings who became more different over a two-year period in their relationships with parents (one sibling grew more intimate with parents, whereas the other grew less so) also became more positive in their relationships with one another. Inconsistent with deidentification theory, however, Whiteman and colleagues (Whiteman & Christiansen, 2008; Whiteman et al., 2007a) found that differentiation dynamics were more prevalent in sibling dyads characterized by less warmth and greater conflict.

One potential explanation for such inconsistencies is that deidentification dynamics and sibling relationship qualities are related nonlinearly. For example, a small degree of differentiation may serve to reduce competition and rivalry, but also maintain shared interests and activities in other domains, thereby promoting warmth and connectedness. Differentiation across too many domains, however, may distance siblings to the point that they fail to engage in shared activities and thus elevate the risk of conflict and distance. Clearly more research is needed to elucidate whether and how deidentification processes relate to one or more domains of sibling relationship qualities.

Longitudinal research is also required to explore the developmental implications of sibling deidentification theory, in particular, the premise that sibling deidentification leads to more harmonious and less conflictual sibling relationships at all points in development. For example, it is possible that deidentification dynamics may be especially prevalent during adolescence, when issues of identity are particularly salient (McHale et al., 2001). Consequently, relationship improvement may not be detected until late adolescence or early adulthood.

Social Learning and Sibling Similarities

In addition to shared genetic (biological siblings share 50 percent of their genetic makeup on average) and shared environmental explanations for sibling similarities, a set of theories (Bandura, 1977; Patterson, 1984) proposes social learning mechanisms, such as modeling, reinforcement, and opportunity provision, as a basis for why siblings develop and exhibit similarities in their personal qualities and behaviors. In general, most social learning theories suggest that in addition to learning through their own behaviors and actions, individuals form ideas about and learn new behaviors through the observation of others.

Bandura (1977) posited several necessary conditions for observational learning to occur. First, a model must possess salient qualities that attract attention in order for imitation to occur. One of the most important determinants of whether a model will attract another person's attention is the frequency of contact with the model. Individuals who are regularly encountered provide more opportunities for observation, and hence their behaviors may be learned more thoroughly. Because youth spend so much time with their siblings (McHale & Crouter, 1996; Updegraff, McHale, Whiteman, Thayer, & Delgado, 2005), they are potentially very salient models. Bandura also suggested that models will attract an individual's attention if they possess attractive qualities, such as power, mastery, and nurturance. Of relevance to the review here is that older siblings may well possess power and mastery in more domains—given that they are older and more advanced developmentally—and nurturance—given their roles as teachers and caregivers—in the eyes of a younger sibling, making them more likely models for younger siblings to observe and imitate than vice versa. Research and theory on modeling also suggest that models who are similar to the self are more likely to be imitated. As such, same-sex siblings are thought to be more powerful models than opposite-sex siblings (Rowe & Gulley, 1992).

Second, an individual must have the motivation to produce the learned behavior. According to Bandura (1977), a behavior can be learned by observation of a model; however, in order for it to be performed, motivation must be evident, and performance of observed behavior is determined by expectations of reinforcement. Importantly, older siblings may be sources of both vicarious and direct reinforcement. For example, Patterson and colleagues (Patterson, 1984; Patterson, Dishion, & Bank, 1984) demonstrated that the development and maintenance of aggressive and coercive behaviors in adolescence is related to patterns of modeling of and reinforcement by an older sibling. In fact, in studying clinical samples, Patterson and colleagues labeled the sibling relationship a "training ground" for antisocial and aggressive behavior because younger siblings were observed to learn these behaviors in accordance with older siblings' reinforcement and modeling of aversive behaviors. In their work with nationally representative samples, Rowe and colleagues (Rowe & Gulley, 1992; Rodgers, Rowe, & Harris, 1992) identified two additional ways in which older siblings may further social learning processes: by providing the materials and settings in which siblings engage in shared behaviors and by providing a network of potential friends who can act as models and partners for new behaviors.

With social learning models as their base, many researchers have explored whether and how older siblings' behaviors are related to their younger siblings' expression of similar behaviors. A complete review of this literature is beyond the scope of this chapter; thus, we limit our review to similarities between siblings in the areas of substance use, sexual behavior, and aggression.

Alcohol and Substance Use. A growing literature on adolescents' alcohol and drug use documents that older siblings' substance use is a

NEW DIRECTIONS FOR CHILD AND ADOLESCENT DEVELOPMENT • DOI: 10.1002/cd

strong predictor of younger siblings' use (Fagan & Najman, 2005; Windle, 2000). In fact, several studies examining the relative contributions of family and peer influences on adolescents' alcohol and substance use have indicated that the magnitude of sibling influence is greater than parental influences (Ary, Tildesley, Hops, & Andrews, 1993; Fagan & Najman, 2005; Windle, 2000) and on a par with peer influences (Brook, Whiteman, Gordon, & Brook, 1990). Furthermore, behavioral genetic investigations of adolescents' substance use patterns have indicated that sibling linkages are above and beyond the contributions of genetic similarity (McGue, Sharma, & Benson, 1996; Rende, Slomkowski, Lloyd-Richardson, & Niaura, 2005). In short, the accumulating evidence suggests that older siblings make a unique contribution to their younger brothers' and sisters' developing substance use attitudes and behaviors. To date, however, studies of sibling influence on adolescents' substance use have been limited by the fact that they do not measure sibling influence processes directly, but rather invoke them as post hoc explanations for observed similarities between siblings.

Sibling similarities in substance use may be explained in part through social learning theory. For example, through vicarious learning, younger siblings may learn about the availability of substances and the consequences of substance use; such learning may increase the likelihood that substance use will be imitated. Researchers in this area (D'Amico & Fromme, 1997; Needle et al., 1986) have suggested that before actually engaging in substance use themselves, adolescents may develop outcome expectancies for alcohol and drug use based on the consequences of substance use by older siblings, and that in many cases, expectancies are positive. In addition to acting as models for younger siblings, supporting an opportunity provision hypothesis, research shows that older siblings are often a source of substances and that they act as co-users of those substances (Needle et al., 1986), thereby leading to further behavioral similarity between siblings. As we suggest below, in order to elucidate the mechanisms responsible for the linkages between siblings' attitudes and behaviors, research designs must be improved to explicitly measure these processes of influence.

Sexual Activity. Studies on adolescent sexual activity and teenage pregnancy highlight that older siblings' sexual behaviors are important predictors of younger siblings' attitudes and activities (East, Felice, & Morgan, 1993; East & Kiernan, 2001). For example, having an older sister who is a teen mother is associated with younger sisters' more permissive attitudes toward sex and childbearing (East & Kiernan, 2001), more intentions for sex in the future, greater likelihood of engaging in sexual intercourse at an early age (East et al., 1993; Rodgers & Rowe, 1988), and a greater likelihood of becoming pregnant themselves (East & Jacobson, 2001). For younger brothers, having a sister who is a teen mother is related to an earlier age of first intercourse (East & Kiernan, 2001). Furthermore, adolescents with sexually active older siblings are more likely to have engaged in sexual intercourse than adolescents with nonsexually active older siblings (Rodgers & Rowe, 1988).

Several theoretical models have been proposed to explain how older siblings may influence younger siblings' sexual activity. First, social learning mechanisms include the transmission of beliefs about sexual activity and childbearing from an older adolescent sibling to a younger adolescent sibling. For example, older siblings may be sources of information regarding sexual activities and also exert pressure to perform those activities. As a result, younger siblings may be more informed at earlier ages and may also feel greater pressure to actually engage in those behaviors. Second, in addition to being models and sources of information, Rodgers and Rowe (1988) and Rodgers et al. (1992) suggest that older siblings may play another role in their younger siblings' sexual activities: that of potential matchmaker. For example, older siblings may introduce their younger brothers and sisters to potential companions who are older and possibly more experienced sexually, leading to increased risk for earlier sexual activity. This dynamic may be especially important for opposite-sex sibling pairs.

Aggression. Studies of aggression and antisocial behavior document that sibling conflict explains unique variance in adolescents' antisocial behaviors, above and beyond the effects of parenting and parent-child relationships (Bank, Burraston, & Snyder, 2004; Garcia, Shaw, Winslow, & Yaggi, 2000). In contrast to research examining similarity between siblings' substance use and sexual activity, mechanisms for sibling similarity in the domain of aggression have been better identified and tested. In clinical samples, Patterson and colleagues (Patterson, 1984; Patterson et al., 1984) found support for a sibling-trainer hypothesis in which older siblings act as models for and train younger siblings to be increasingly antisocial, which ultimately leads to behavioral similarity.

Using a normative sample of adolescents, Slomkowski, Rende, Conger, Simons, and Conger (2001) examined whether qualities of the sibling relationship related to sibling similarities in delinquent behaviors. Consistent with both a sibling trainer hypothesis and reinforcement principles, they found that similarity in delinquency was highest in highly coercive relationships, suggesting that siblings reinforce one another's aggressive and antisocial behaviors, and highest under conditions of sibling warmth in brother-brother pairs, suggesting that individuals may be more likely to imitate models who are similar to them and with whom they have a close relationship.

New Directions for Research

Although an abundance of literature documents sibling similarity, more research needs to be conducted to elucidate the mechanisms that create these similarities. With the exception of Patterson and colleagues' work on similarities in aggressive behaviors, most research on sibling similarities has relied on correlational designs. As such, we are limited to post hoc explanations for why siblings show similarities, such as social learning mechanisms. Although there are difficulties inherent in testing social learning theories in areas such as substance use, sexuality, and delinquency because of the inability to both manipulate these behaviors in the laboratory and tease apart the effects of shared genes, shared environments, and social learning processes, future research can improve existing methods in the following ways.

First, researchers should measure social learning processes directly, for example, by asking respondents how much they want or try to be like their siblings. In this way, the connection between social learning mechanisms and sibling similarity may be illuminated. For example, using two different measurement strategies, Whiteman et al. (2007a, 2007b) found that siblings' reports of modeling were indeed connected to similarities in their interests, attitudes, and behaviors. Consistent with social learning principles, cluster analyses revealed that 43 percent of second-borns reported intentionally modeling their older siblings (Whiteman et al., 2007a).

Because these findings suggested that modeling processes were not domain specific, Whiteman and colleagues (2007b) designed a second measure to assess modeling processes more globally. Specifically, they asked second-borns to "rate the degree to which their siblings set an example for their behavior, encouraged them to participate in activities, and included them in activities" (p. 966). They found that after controlling for relationship quality, second-born siblings were more similar to their older brothers and sisters when they reported a high degree of modeling and their older sibling was engaged, competent, or interested in a particular domain.

Second, researchers can follow the lead of Rowe and Gulley (1992), Slomkowski et al. (2001), and Rende and colleagues (2005) to examine how family structural characteristics and sibling relationship qualities relate to sibling similarities. Because social learning theory posits that imitation should be greater in same-sex dyads as well as in relationships that are characterized by greater warmth and nurturance, future work can examine whether patterns of correlation are stronger in these contexts and provide a stronger basis for inferring social learning processes.

Third, future research needs to move beyond the current focus on risky behavior and delinquency and explore other domains of adjustment and development. For example, Tucker, Updegraff, McHale, and Crouter (1999) found that youth model their older siblings in the area of empathy. Future research should continue to investigate the role of social learning mechanisms in other more positive domains of behavior, including siblings' propensities to emulate each other's leadership, teaching, sharing, and caregiving behaviors.

Finally, the literature is limited in that with few exceptions (McHale et al., 2001; Trim, Leuthe, & Chassin, 2006; Whiteman & Christiansen, 2008), most studies have examined top-down models of socialization. That is, they have focused on how older siblings serve as models or foils for their younger brothers and sisters. In contrast, the ways in which younger siblings influence their older brothers and sisters are largely unknown and represent an important area for future research. For example, bottom-up dynamics may be especially important during adolescence, when older and younger siblings' cognitive and physical abilities are more alike.

Conclusion

The literature on sibling similarities and differences suggests that siblings are indeed influential in each other's lives; however, the magnitude and direction of that influence is not always clear. In order to disentangle how siblings influence one another, mechanisms of similarity (social learning) need to be considered concurrently with mechanisms related to sibling differences (deidentification). Although these forces are posed as independent processes, whether they operate independently or in concert with one another is largely unknown. Given the complexity of studying competing dynamics, the use of multiple approaches—qualitative, quantitative, person oriented, and others—may yield the greatest evidence of when and under what contexts these phenomena emerge and operate.

In addition, the domains and developmental periods in which these processes operate need greater exploration. For example, given that sibling deidentification is posed as both a conscious and unconscious process, it is possible that differentiation dynamics may be particularly prevalent in trait-like domains such as personality and temperament, whereas modeling dynamics may be more likely when examining youth's activities and behaviors. Furthermore, the extent to which modeling and differentiation processes vary as a function of a youth's age or developmental status is also unknown. A body of work on social learning highlights that modeling behaviors occur primarily in childhood and adolescence. Because deidentification dynamics have been largely tested in adolescence and early adulthood, whether and how these dynamics operate in early and middle childhood is unknown. With recent statistical advances, including growth curve modeling, researchers can test developmental hypotheses such as when sibling differences emerge and how they change during childhood and adolescence.

Given that sibling relationships operate within a larger family system, it is also important that future work examine how parents' beliefs, expectations, and values relate to siblings' socialization and adjustment. For example, in families where conformity to parents' rules and expectations is stressed (for example, with authoritarian parenting), social learning processes may be especially adaptive and sibling similarities may be accentuated. Furthermore, because most work on sibling influences has been conducted with white, middle-class samples, our understanding of how these processes of socialization vary across socioeconomic strata and cultures is limited. Future research would benefit from the examination of sibling influence dynamics in more diverse contexts where siblings' roles and expectations may differ as a result of cultural belief, such as familism (Updegraff et al., 2005).

Finally, research that provides a greater understanding of the contexts and correlates of sibling influence will have important implications for practitioners and parents alike. Although interventions involving siblings are rare (Kramer, 2004), siblings represent important targets for future interventions, and understanding how and when siblings may model as opposed to deidentify from one another may be especially important. Ultimately, by synthesizing divergent theories and testing competing processes of influence, researchers will be better positioned to explicate how brothers and sisters affect each other's development.

References

Ary, D. V., Tildesley, E., Hops, H., & Andrews, J. (1993). The influence of parent, sibling, and peer modeling and attitudes on adolescent use of alcohol. *International Journal of the Addictions, 28,* 853–880.

Bandura, A. (1977). *Social learning theory.* Upper Saddle River, NJ: Prentice Hall.

Bank, L., Burraston, B., & Snyder, J. (2004). Sibling conflict and ineffective parenting as predictors of adolescent boys' antisocial behavior and peer difficulties: Additive and interactional effects. *Journal of Research on Adolescence, 14,* 99–125.

Brody, G. H. (1998). Sibling relationship quality: Its causes and consequences. *Annual Review of Psychology, 49,* 1–24.

Brody, G. H., & Murry, V. M. (2001). Sibling socialization of competence in rural, single-parent African American families. *Journal of Marriage and the Family, 63*(4), 996–1008.

Brook, J. S., Whiteman, M., Gordon, A. S., & Brook, D. W. (1990). The role of older brothers in younger brothers' drug use viewed in the context of parent and peer influences. *Journal of Genetic Psychology, 151,* 59–75.

D'Amico, E. J., & Fromme, K. (1997). Health risk behaviors of adolescent and young adult siblings. *Health Psychology, 16,* 426–432.

Dunn, J., Brown, J., Slomkowski, C., Tesla, C., & Youngblade, L. (1991). Young children's understanding of other people's feelings and beliefs: Individual differences and their antecedents. *Child Development, 62,*1352–1366.

Dunn, J., & Plomin, R. (1990). *Separate lives: Why siblings are so different.* New York: Basic Books.

East, P. L., Felice, M. E., & Morgan, M. C. (1993). Sisters' and girlfriends' sexual and childbearing behavior: Effects on early adolescent girls' sexual outcomes. *Journal of Marriage and the Family, 55,* 953–963.

East, P. L., & Jacobson, L. J. (2001). The younger siblings of teenage mothers: A follow-up of their pregnancy risk. *Developmental Psychology, 37,* 254–264.

East, P. L., & Kiernan, E. A. (2001). Risks among youths who have multiple sisters who were adolescent parents. *Family Planning Perspectives, 33,* 75–80.

Fagan, A. A., & Najman, J. M. (2005). The relative contributions of parental and sibling substance use to adolescent tobacco, alcohol, and other drug use. *Journal of Drug Issues, 35,* 869–883.

Feinberg, M. E., & Hetherington, E. M. (2000). Sibling differentiation in adolescence: Implications for behavioral genetic theory. *Child Development, 71,* 1512–1524.

Feinberg, M. E., McHale, S. M., Crouter, A. C., & Cumsille, P. (2003). Sibling differentiation: Sibling and parent relationship trajectories in adolescence. *Child Development, 74,* 1245–1260.

Feinberg, M. E., Neiderhiser, J. M., Simmens, S., Reiss, D., & Hetherington, E. M. (2000). Sibling comparison of differential treatment in adolescence: Gender, self-esteem, and emotionality as mediators of the parenting-adjustment association. *Child Development*, 71, 1611–1628.

Festinger, L. A. (1954). A theory of social comparison processes. *Human Relations*, 7, 117–140.

Garcia, M. M., Shaw, D. S., Winslow, E. B., & Yaggi, K. E. (2000). Destructive sibling conflict and the development of conduct problems in young boys. *Developmental Psychology*, 36, 44–53.

Grotevant, H. (1978). Sibling constellations and sex-typing of interests in adolescence. *Child Development*, 49, 540–542.

Katz, L. F., Kramer, L., & Gottman, J. M. (1992). Conflict and emotions in marital, sibling, and peer relationships. In W. W. Hartup & C. U. Shantz (Eds.), *Conflict in child and adolescent development* (pp. 122–149). Cambridge: Cambridge University Press.

Kramer, L. (2004). Experimental interventions in sibling relations. In R. D. Conger, F. O. Lorenz, & K. A. S. Wickrama (Eds.), *Continuity and change in family relations: Theory, methods, and empirical findings* (pp. 345–382). Mahwah, NJ: Erlbaum.

Leventhal, G. S. (1970). Influence of brothers and sisters on sex-role behavior. *Journal of Personality and Social Psychology*, 16, 452–465.

McGue, M., Sharma, A., & Benson, P. (1996). Parent and sibling influences on adolescent alcohol use and misuse: Evidence from a U.S. adoption cohort. *Journal of Studies on Alcohol*, 57, 8–18.

McHale, S. M., & Crouter, A. C. (1996). The family contexts of children's sibling relationships. In G. H. Brody (Ed.), *Sibling relationships: Their causes and consequences* (pp. 173–195). Norwood, NJ: Ablex.

McHale, S. M., Updegraff, K. A., Helms-Erikson, H., & Crouter, A. C. (2001). Sibling influences on gender development in middle childhood and early adolescence: A longitudinal study. *Developmental Psychology*, 37, 115–215.

Needle, R., McCubbin, H., Wilson, M., Reineck, R., Lazar, A., & Mederer, H. (1986). Interpersonal influences in adolescent drug use: The role of older siblings, parents, and peers. *International Journal of the Addictions*, 21, 739–766.

Patterson, G. R. (1984). Siblings: Fellow travelers in coercive family processes. In R. J. Blanchard (Ed.), *Advances in the study of aggression* (pp. 173–215). Orlando, FL: Academic Press.

Patterson, G. R., Dishion, T. J., & Bank, L. (1984). Family interaction: A process model of deviancy training. *Aggressive Behavior*, 10, 253–267.

Plomin, R., & Daniels, D. (1987). Why are children in the same family so different from one another? *Behavioural and Brain Sciences*, 10, 1–16.

Rende, R., Slomkowski, C., Lloyd-Richardson, E., & Niaura, R. (2005). Sibling effects on substance use in adolescence: Social contagion and genetic relatedness. *Journal of Family Psychology*, 19, 611–618.

Rodgers, J. L., & Rowe, D. C. (1988). Influence of siblings on adolescent sexual behavior. *Developmental Psychology*, 24, 722–728.

Rodgers, J. L., Rowe, D. C., & Harris, D. F. (1992). Sibling differences in adolescent sexual behavior: Inferring process models from family composition patterns. *Journal of Marriage and the Family*, 54, 142–152.

Rowe, D., & Gulley, B. (1992). Sibling effects on substance abuse and delinquency. *Criminology*, 30, 217–233.

Schachter, F. F., Gilutz, G., Shore, E., & Adler, M. (1978). Sibling deidentification judged by mothers: Cross validation and developmental studies. *Child Development*, 49, 543–546.

Schachter, F. F., Shore, E., Feldman-Rotman, S., Marquis, R. E., & Campbell, S. (1976). Sibling deidentification. *Developmental Psychology*, 12, 418–427.

Schachter, F. F., & Stone, R. K. (1985). Difficult sibling, easy sibling: Temperament and the within-family environment. *Child Development*, 56, 1335–1344.

Slomkowski, C., Rende, R., Conger, K. J., Simons, R. L., & Conger, R. D. (2001). Sisters, brothers, and delinquency: Evaluating social influence during early and middle adolescence. *Child Development, 72,* 271–283.

Sulloway, F. J. (1996). *Born to rebel: Birth order, family dynamics, and creative lives.* New York: Pantheon Books.

Tesser, A. (1980). Self-esteem maintenance in family dynamics. *Journal of Personality and Social Psychology, 39,* 77–91.

Trim, R. S., Leuthe, E., & Chassin, L. (2006). Sibling influence on alcohol use in a young adult, high-risk sample. *Journal of Studies on Alcohol, 67*(3), 391–398.

Tucker, C. J., Updegraff, K. A., McHale, S. M., & Crouter, A. C. (1999). Older siblings as socializers of younger siblings' empathy. *Journal of Early Adolescence, 19,* 176–198.

Updegraff, K. A., McHale, S. M., Whiteman, S. D., Thayer, S. M., & Delgado, M. Y. (2005). Adolescent sibling relationships in Mexican American families: Exploring the role of familism. *Journal of Family Psychology, 19,* 512–522.

Whiteman, S. D., & Christiansen, A. (2008). Processes of sibling influence in adolescence: Individual and family correlates. *Family Relations, 57,* 24–34.

Whiteman, S. D., McHale, S. M., & Crouter, A. C. (2007a). Competing processes of sibling influence: Observational learning and sibling deidentification. *Social Development, 16,* 642–661.

Whiteman, S. D., McHale, S. M., & Crouter, A. C. (2007b). Explaining sibling similarities: Perceptions of sibling influences. *Journal of Youth and Adolescence, 36,* 963–972.

Windle, M. (2000). Parental, sibling, and peer influences on adolescent substance use and alcohol problems. *Applied Developmental Science, 4,* 98–110.

SHAWN D. WHITEMAN is an assistant professor of family studies in the Department of Child Development and Family Studies at Purdue University, West Lafayette, Indiana. E-mail: sdwhitem@purdue.edu.

JULIA M. BECERRA is a doctoral candidate in the Department of Child Development and Family Studies at Purdue University, West Lafayette, Indiana. E-mail: jbecerra@purdue.edu.

SARAH E. KILLOREN is an instructor in the Department of Human Development and Family Studies at Colorado State University, Fort Collins. E-mail: Sarah.Killoren@colostate.edu.

Conger, K. J., Stocker, C., & McGuire, S. (2009). Sibling socialization: The effects of stressful life events and experiences. In L. Kramer & K. J. Conger (Eds.), *Siblings as agents of socialization. New Directions for Child and Adolescent Development, 126,* 45–60. San Francisco: Jossey-Bass.

Sibling Socialization: The Effects of Stressful Life Events and Experiences

Katherine J. Conger, Clare Stocker, Shirley McGuire

Abstract

Stressful life events and experiences may disrupt the typical day-to-day interactions between sisters and brothers that provide the foundation of sibling socialization. This chapter examines four experiences that may affect patterns of sibling interaction: parental marital conflict, parental divorce and remarriage, foster care placement, and a sibling's developmental disability. We propose a model to guide future research on sibling socialization in distressed families and special populations in which qualities of the sibling relationship moderate the effects of stressful life experiences on child and family adjustment. © Wiley Periodicals, Inc.

We thank Wendy Little for assistance with this chapter.

A cross all cultural settings, older siblings frequently serve as teacher, advisor, role model, playmate, caregiver, and confidant for their younger sisters and brothers (see Weisner, 1989; Zukow-Goldring, 2002). However, the research that has established these processes of sibling socialization has typically focused on the development of children in normative, healthy family contexts (see Dunn, 2007; Chapter Three, this volume). Less attention has been devoted to examining the role of siblings in families facing adverse conditions, such as chronic or terminal illness, mental retardation, physical disabilities, or challenging experiences such as poverty, death of a parent, or marital conflict. Thousands of families face stressful conditions or experiences each day, yet the individual stories of these families are not often represented in research on normative mechanisms of socialization (Hodapp, Glidden, & Kaiser, 2005). This chapter explores whether the basic mechanisms of sibling socialization are the same in stressed and nonstressed (that is, normative) families, recognizing that different forms of socialization may emerge to accommodate specific events and conditions. The chapter concludes by proposing a model to guide future research on sibling socialization in distressed families and special populations.

In line with Whiteman, Becerra, and Killoren in Chapter Three in this volume, we propose that social learning is one of the primary ways in which sibling socialization takes place. Furthermore, we contend that socialization processes should be examined within the ecological contexts of family, community, and culture (McGuire & Shanahan, in press; Parke & Buriel, 1998; Chapter Two, this volume). Finally, due to the lifelong nature of sibling relationships, we also employ a life course perspective (see Conger, 2008; Elder, 1998) in proposing that turning points or transitional events may alter the course of an individual's development or the course of important social relationships. These transitions may be normative events or developmental markers, such as starting school, developing close friendships, gaining pubertal maturity, and getting a driver's license. Transitions may also be nonnormative events, such as chronic illness, disability, or sudden death, that serve as unexpected turning points for individuals and their siblings.

Family Stressors and Sibling Socialization

Typically developing siblings learn from one another through imitation during everyday play and family activities, and these interactions provide ongoing opportunities to acquire social, emotional, and behavioral competencies. Much of this learning takes place through observation and imitation (that is, social learning) as younger siblings emulate and try to keep up with more skilled older brothers and sisters. Research suggests that it is both the cooperative play and the conflictual interactions that assist siblings in learning new skills and defining themselves as individuals (see Brody, 1998; Howe & Ross, 1990; Kramer, 2004; Schacter & Stone, 1987). Even in adulthood and old age, siblings continue to define themselves and measure their success in comparison to their siblings (Conley, 2004; Connidis & Campbell, 1995; Milevsky, 2005). For some, however, the normative social processes of imitation, social play, conflict management, and other everyday activities are hindered by barriers such as mental retardation, physical disabilities, illness, or other negative life events that disrupt normal family functioning and relationships (see Gath, 1992; Sakai, Sugawara, Maeshiro, Amou, & Takuma et al., 2002; Stoneman & Berman, 1993).

This chapter describes the ways in which life experiences may influence sibling relationships. We focus on four stressful family experiences that may alter socialization processes and sibling relationships: parental marital conflict, parental divorce and remarriage, foster care placement, and a sibling's developmental disability.

Marital Conflict

In some respects, marital conflict, and for some, subsequent separation and divorce, might be considered almost normative due to the large numbers of children who are affected at some point in the life course (Amato, 2000; Cherlin, 2005). However, there is not a one-to-one correspondence between marital conflict and poor sibling relationships. Research has revealed the complexity of the impact of marital conflict on children and their sibling relationships (Harold, Fincham, Obsborne, & Conger, 1997; Jenkins, 1992; McGuire & Shanahan, in press; Stocker, Ahmed, & Stall, 1997). These studies lead us to expect that conflict between parents can influence sibling socialization in two basic ways.

First, marital conflict can have an impact on each child's personal adjustment, which can shape the quality of sibling relationships. Numerous studies document associations between parental marital quality and children's adjustment (Davies & Cummings, 1994; Grych & Fincham, 1990; Simons & Associates, 1996); however, only recently have studies considered how this association may vary among children in the same family. Some aspects of marital quality may be experienced in similar ways by different siblings; for instance, the frequency of parental disputes tends to be linked to externalizing problems in all siblings in a family (Jenkins, Dunn, Rasbash, O'Connor, & Simpson, 2005). However, individual siblings may experience marital conflict differently from one another. These unique experiences and perceptions may be linked with differential adjustment to marital conflict (Richmond & Stocker, 2006; Skopp, McDonald, Manke, & Jouriles, 2005).

Second, marital conflict can affect the nature of the sibling relationship as children imitate parents' hostile, coercive interactions and perhaps experience the spillover of hostility to increased parent-child antagonism. By witnessing aggressive interparental conflict, children may infer that this form of behavior is an acceptable way to interact with siblings. In fact, the congruency hypothesis suggests that children living with parents who are in conflict are at higher risk for experiencing conflictual sibling relationships (Brody, Stoneman, McCoy, & Forehand, 1992; Conger & Conger, 1996; Stocker & Youngblade, 1999). It is important to note, however, that the direction of marital and sibling associations may also travel from siblings to parents' marriages.

As most parents know, sibling conflict can be extremely irritating and stressful and can exacerbate marital conflict. Consistent with family systems theory, family relationships are interconnected and do not operate in isolation (Cox & Paley, 1997). Antagonistic marital functioning may spill over, negatively affecting the quality of parent-child relationships (Erel, Margolin, & John, 1998), which may in turn promote greater negativity in sibling relationships (Stocker & Youngblade, 1999).

In contrast, there is also evidence suggesting that siblings in disharmonious homes may draw closer and provide support for one another during times of adversity (Bank & Kahn, 1982; Jenkins, 1992). Jenkins found that children in homes with marital conflict were more likely to develop hostile relationships with their siblings (see also Conger & Conger, 1996). However, Jenkins also found evidence for protective effects: children who had very close sibling relationships demonstrated lower levels of symptoms, even in disharmonious homes.

What could lead to these different patterns of findings? Why in some cases are siblings able to maintain positive and supportive relationships that work as buffers against the link between marital conflict and adjustment problems? It is possible that the match of siblings' personalities or a history of especially supportive sibling relationships that predate parents' marital conflict may enable children to turn to siblings for support when coping with the stressors accompanying interparental conflict.

Parental Divorce and Remarriage

Family disruptions such as divorce may erect barriers to typical sibling socialization and impose constraints on developing and maintaining positive relations between siblings (Stocker & Youngblade, 1999). Divorce may also lead to shifting alliances between or among siblings. For example, children may align with different parents to ensure that both parents have a child "in their corner" (see Christensen & Margolin, 1988). As individual children identify with and support a different parent, emotional separations may grow between siblings.

According to Amato (2000) and others, divorce is a critical life event that requires adjustment on the part of both children and adults. Many studies show that sibling relationships in divorced families are more hostile, less supportive, and more distant across the life span compared to sibling relationships in nondivorced families (MacKinnon, 1989; Milevsky, 2004; Panish & Stricker, 2001; Poortman & Voorpostel, 2009; Riggio, 2001; Sheehan, Darlington, Noller, & Feeney, 2004). Consistent with both family systems

(Cox & Paley, 1997) and congruency (Conger & Conger, 1996) frameworks, sibling relationships deteriorate in response to the high parental conflict and stress that occurs throughout the entire divorce transition.

Changes to the sibling bond may not end with parental divorce. Nearly half of current marriages are remarriages (Amato, 2000), and siblings with divorced parents experience new socialization opportunities and challenges when their parents remarry and new stepfamily relationships are formed (Coleman, Ganong, & Fine, 2001; Hetherington, 1988). Unless their relationship has been repaired, the additional requirement of forging new and often complex stepparent and stepsibling relationships may exacerbate existing hostility and resentment between siblings and could interfere with the establishment of positive stepsibling relationships (Hetherington, 1988).

The merging of households and families may produce further resentment, especially in teenagers, as children are sometimes required to share bedrooms and bathrooms, along with sharing the affection and loyalties of parents and grandparents. In some cases, custody and visitation schedules create situations in which stepsiblings interact only during weekends and holidays, making positive socialization opportunities scarce. In addition, continued interparental conflict after divorce further reduces the quality of sibling relationships (MacKinnon, 1989).

There is evidence, however, that a supportive sibling relationship may serve as a buffer during the stress of divorce and remarriage (Hetherington, 1988; Kempton, Armistead, Wierson, & Forehand, 1991). Warm and supportive sibling relationships may compensate for the lack of attention children receive from quarreling or distant parents. Older siblings may move from secondary caregivers to primary parenting figures in younger siblings' lives. The gender constellation of siblings in divorced and remarried families is an important factor as sisters provide more comfort to their siblings, particularly to other sisters (Anderson, 1999; Anderson & Rice, 1992; Gass, Jenkins, & Dunn, 2007).

In conclusion, the challenges of marital conflict, divorce, and remarriage exert complex influences on sibling socialization. In most cases, marital conflict, divorce, and remarriage are linked to increased sibling conflict and less supportive sibling relationships. However, in other families, sibling relationships may also play a positive and protective role in the face of family instability and marital conflict. Siblings who are able to maintain a solid relationship through these transitions may provide critical stability that each can use in the future when confronted with stress and when forming new intimate relationships.

Foster Care Placement

A family disruption that affects far fewer children than does divorce, but has the potential for lifelong effects (see Shlonsky, Bellamy, Elkins, & Ashare, 2005), is placement in foster care. Approximately 70 percent of the 800,000 children in foster care in the United States have at least one sibling in care (U.S. Department of Health and Human Services, 2008), and about half of these siblings are placed in separate homes. This is true despite the fact that siblings may be crucial agents of socialization who provide one another with a sense of connection and emotional continuity when children are separated from parents and other family members (Tarren-Sweeney & Hazell, 2005).

In practice, siblings are frequently placed apart for reasons ranging from concern about the safety of one sibling (especially in cases of physical or sexual abuse) to the unavailability of foster homes that can accommodate larger sibling groups (Leathers, 2005; Linares, 2006). Whereas sibling conflict is fairly normative, it is one factor that is considered when making placement decisions; siblings exposed to high levels of conflict or family violence are at higher risk of directing aggression toward one another (Bank, Patterson, & Reid, 1996; Patterson, 1986). Separate placements protect more vulnerable siblings from sibling bullying or sibling violence (Linares, 2006). Furthermore, the ability of foster parents to provide more positive, and less rejecting, care to these at-risk siblings needs to be considered when examining the long-term effects of placing siblings together or apart.

In general, more positive outcomes, such as fewer emotional and behavioral problems, are found for siblings who are placed together in foster care (Herrick & Piccus, 2005; Smith, 1998). For very young children, an older sibling may serve as an important attachment figure (Stewart, 1983; Teti & Ablard, 1989), facilitating socialization of the younger child as well as promoting a sense of self-identity for the older sibling. Importantly, Leathers (2005) found that children placed with siblings were less likely to experience placement disruption and more likely to experience either permanent placement or reunification with biological parents (see Webster, Shlonsky, Shaw, & Brookhart, 2005).

When siblings are placed together, one concern is that they may band together and not become integrated into the foster family (Leathers, 2005). A related concern is that older siblings are expected to be the primary caregivers for younger siblings (parentification). Social workers and foster parents worry that older siblings who assume this type of caregiver role lose the opportunity to be children themselves, and precautions must be taken to alleviate these responsibilities (see Herrick & Piccus, 2005). However, for many children, a placement with siblings may be a positive experience that is consistent with their cultural and family expectations (see Begun, 1995; Depp, 1983). For those children, the primary caregiver role may provide a sense of security and of being needed. In fact, some older siblings grieve the loss of the caregiver role after separation from their younger siblings (Herrick & Piccus, 2005). Some children who are not allowed to continue the role of caregiver for younger siblings may have poorer outcomes, such as feelings of guilt and reduced self-esteem (see Kaplan, Hennon, & Ade-Ridder, 1993). In a survey of caseworkers, the most commonly cited factors in making decisions to place siblings together were alleviating the sense of loss that comes with parental separation and preserving sibling support (Smith, 1998).

The sibling bond may serve as a critical source of resiliency for children in foster care who must leave the system after they reach the age of eighteen. For example, older siblings who enter college can assist younger siblings coming behind (see Milevksy, 2005). Older siblings may provide resources such as a place to live and advice about the world of work that may help a younger sibling learn the skills needed to get started (see Conger & Little, in press).

In summary, maintaining positive sibling relationships throughout childhood and adolescence may make it easier to accomplish the tasks of adulthood (Cicirelli, 1992; Conger, Bryant, & Brennom, 2004; Goetting, 1986), and this may be especially true for siblings who have grown up in foster care. Despite the fact that placing siblings together may preserve vital social and emotional support, currently only twenty-six states have guidelines in place that take siblings into account when making placement decisions (Herrick & Piccus, 2005).

A Sibling's Developmental Disability

Much of the current research and speculation regarding siblings as socialization agents operate under the implicit assumption that development is progressing normally. While for many children this is the case, not all siblings develop in a typical manner, and many families are challenged to provide a supportive environment for social interaction between siblings. For example, siblings of individuals with developmental delays such as autism or Down syndrome are more likely to experience depression, anxiety, and internalizing and externalizing problems (Brodoff, 1988; Buckley, 2007; Gold, 1993). However, in their meta-analysis, Sharpe and Rossiter (2002) suggest that the negative effects of having a sibling with mental disabilities may be overstated, and research is needed to clarify the long-term effects.

We focus on children with cognitive and socioemotional delays because these delays may be especially stressful for sibling socialization (see Hodapp et al., 2005). Normative mechanisms of sibling socialization, such as imitation, teaching, and reciprocal interactions, may be limited when one child is developing atypically. In particular, developmental delays impose communication challenges, cognitive developmental differences, nonreciprocal behaviors, and other burdens on the typically developing sibling, who often assumes the role of socialization agent, regardless of age and gender composition of the sibship (McHale & Harris, 1992). For example, individuals with impaired social referencing or social competencies, such as those on the autism spectrum (see Gold, 1993; Macks & Reeve, 2007; Rivers & Stoneman, 2003), may have particular difficulty developing satisfying relationships because social interactions are not reciprocal, at least not in the typical sense. The demands placed on the typically developing siblings may be intense because they must use perspective-taking skills to choreograph their communication without any expectation of reciprocation. The intensity of the demands may depend, at least in part, on the level of functioning of the disabled sibling. The family and social context within which these interactions are occurring are also important, as we know that children of siblings with a developmental disability experience a range of reactions: embarrassment, frustration, confusion, feelings of being overlooked or treated differently by parents, and wanting to defend their sibling when they have been treated unjustly, to name just a few (see Gray, 1998; Macks & Reeve, 2007; Morgan, 1988).

So how does sibling socialization occur in these families? The assumption might be that socialization is operating in one direction; that is, the typically developing sibling is socializing the sibling with developmental delays. However, research suggests that typically developing individuals also may gain personal strengths and develop social competencies through their experiences with siblings with disabilities (see Dykens, 2005; Gold, 1993). Grossman (1972) reported that about half of the siblings he interviewed described feeling more open and more tolerant of differences, and they focused on life's larger meaning due to these experiences. Thus, even under difficult circumstances, both older and younger siblings learn from these experiences.

Perhaps typically developing children gain a sense of maturity and an understanding of diversity that exceeds that of children without siblings in need. They may also develop the ability to take another's perspective, exhibit empathy, and protect a vulnerable sibling from dangerous or threatening situations such as those encountered by cognitively challenged siblings. Children develop skills and perspectives from assuming roles as caregiver, teacher, and protector that they can apply to other life challenges. We also suspect that being the recipient of support, caregiving, instruction, and protection from a sibling may be quite meaningful to a child who faces significant developmental challenges. These lessons likely play out over the life course as siblings face the long-term consequences and challenges of caring for individuals with developmental delays in adulthood (see Bigby, 1997; Seltzer, Greenberg, Orsmond, & Lounds, 2005).

Future Directions for Research

This chapter has addressed four stressful experiences that siblings may face during the life course, and a number of questions present themselves as a result of this review. It is clear that while sibling relationships may be negatively affected by challenging life experiences, these same experiences also provide opportunities for positive growth and change. Future research should examine the life events and experiences under which close, supportive sibling relationships lead to better adjustment, as well as those circumstances that are linked with conflictual sibling relationships and adjustment difficulties.

NEW DIRECTIONS FOR CHILD AND ADOLESCENT DEVELOPMENT • DOI: 10.1002/cd

Findings from across a wide variety of fields, including social work, nursing, education, child development, sociology, and psychology, suggest that researchers need a more balanced view of sibling research in which both positive and negative antecedents and outcomes are considered (Conger et al., 2004; Hodapp et al., 2005). In addition, researchers need to more frequently consider studies from outside their own discipline to keep an open mind about what constitutes the full range of sibling life experiences that shape these lifelong relationships and influence individual health and well-being (Connidis, 2001; Gass et al., 2007; McGuire & Shanahan, in press; Zukow-Goldring, 2002). For example, studies from anthropology provide rich descriptions of preschool-age siblings socializing their younger siblings about daily life in their village (see Nuckolls, 1993). Indeed, McGuire and Shanahan (in press) and Weisner (1989) challenge researchers to study siblings across both disciplinary boundaries and cultures. Weisner suggests that we need to take the social ecology of the family and community into account to understand which factors are shaping the ongoing sibling relationship. Weisner (1989) states, "Comparisons of siblings across cultures should situate siblings within their everyday worlds and the local ecology around them and their families" (p. 14).

To stimulate discussions among sibling researchers, we propose a model of sibling socialization (see Figure 4.1) that describes the effect of stressful family experiences on patterns of sibling interaction (arrow A) and how these in turn affect individual adjustment (arrow B) over time. The experiences reviewed in this chapter (marital conflict, divorce and remarriage, foster care placement, and developmental disabilities) have a common theme in that they all create instability and uncertainty for siblings and their families. Instability and uncertainty in turn create pressures on individuals and their sibling relationships that otherwise might not occur. The model proposes that stressful life circumstances have a direct effect on patterns of interaction and opportunities for sibling socialization (arrow A). In addition, parenting behaviors and characteristics may have a direct effect (arrow C) on sibling interactions. For example, marital conflict may have a direct effect, as when siblings imitate the conflictual interactions of their maritally distressed parents. However, parenting may also moderate (arrow E) the link between life experiences and sibling interactions. For example, parents who are nurturant and involved with their children can buffer the negative effects of divorce and similar experiences. In contrast, parents who become harsh and inconsistent during times of stress may exacerbate the potentially negative effects of these life experiences.

The model also considers earlier sibling relationship quality as a predictor of later patterns of interaction (arrow D). For example, siblings who enjoy positive relationships are more likely to maintain prosocial interactions and provide support in the face of family stressors. Furthermore, high-quality sibling relationships may moderate and buffer the deleterious effects of stressful life experiences on later sibling interactions (arrow F). Conversely, poor-quality sibling relationships may intensify the effect of

Figure 4.1. Conceptual Model of the Effect of Challenging Life Experiences on Sibling Socialization

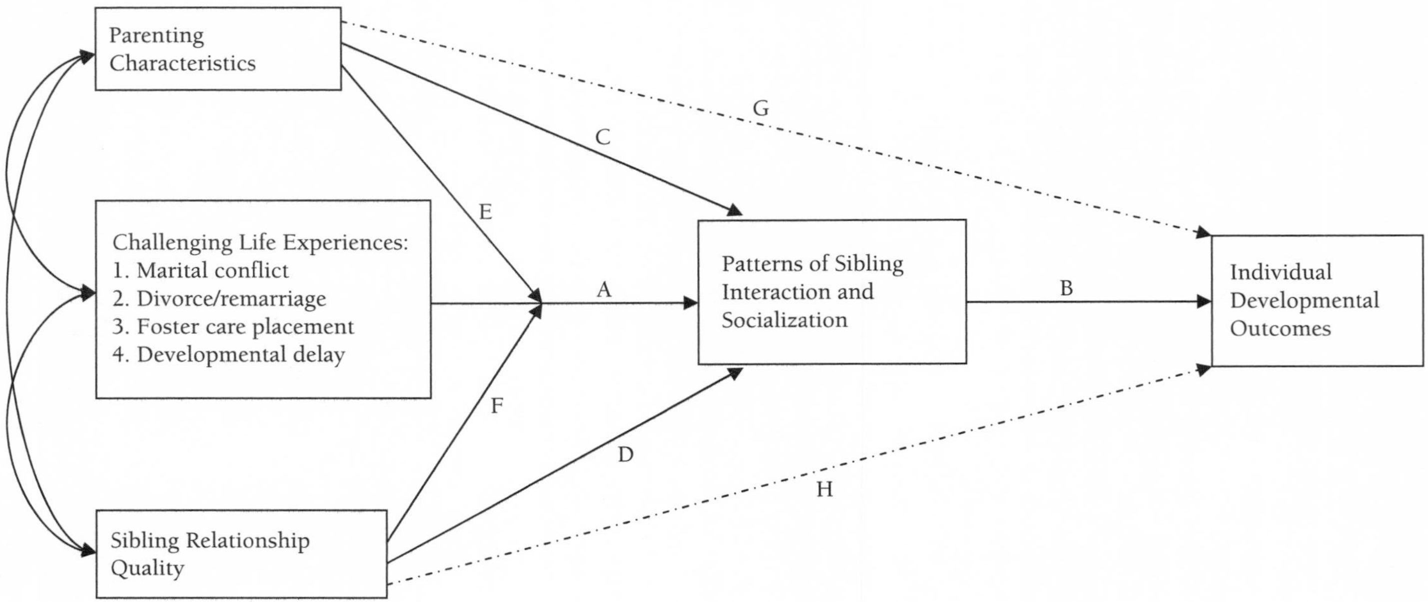

negative experiences on later sibling interactions and thus heighten the risk for adjustment problems. Finally, both parenting and sibling relationship quality may have direct as well as indirect effects through sibling socialization on the developmental outcomes of individual siblings (arrows G and H, respectively).

We further propose that the social processes of the model be viewed within the context of the social network and cultural values and beliefs of the family that may influence the expectations for sibling involvement in one another's lives (McGuire & Shanahan, in press; Weisner, 1993). Although we cannot represent all possible influences on siblings' relationships, our model provides a point of common reference for researchers to use as they develop a more inclusive and comprehensive understanding of the opportunities and constraints for sibling socialization and its impact on individual development throughout the life course.

Conclusion

This examination of sibling socialization reinforces the idea that we need to consider siblings as important sources of support in the face of stressful life events and experiences. It is also clear that we need to study these lifelong relationships in the context of other family relationships (for example, marital and parent-child), as well as in the larger social networks in which families are embedded. Our review found that sibling relationships can thrive when resources such as effective parenting are available to assist siblings to maintain their relationship or suffer when barriers such as separate foster placements exist. Future research should focus on understanding the processes by which stressful life events can lead to positive or negative outcomes for siblings. Researchers, clinicians, and practitioners must work to support sibling relationships that serve as potent agents of socialization, helping children to respond effectively to challenging experiences across the life course.

References

Amato, P. (2000). The consequences of divorce for children. *Journal of Marriage and the Family, 62*, 1269–1287.

Anderson, E. R. (1999). Sibling, half-sibling, and stepsibling relationships in remarried families. In E. M. Hetherington, S. H. Henderson, & D. Reiss (Eds.), Adolescent siblings in stepfamilies: Family functioning and the adolescent adjustment. *Monographs for the Society for Research in Child Development, 64* (Serial No. 259), 1–222.

Anderson, E. R., & Rice, A. M. (1992). Sibling relationships during remarriage. In E. M. Hetherington & W. G. Clingempeel (Eds.), Coping with marital transitions: A family systems perspective. *Monographs for the Society for Research in Child Development, 57* (Serial No. 227), 1–242.

Bank, L., Patterson, G. R., & Reid, J. B. (1996). Negative sibling interaction patterns as predictors of later adjustment processes in young male adolescents. In G. H. Brody (Ed.), *Sibling relationships: Their causes and consequences* (pp. 197–229). Norwood, NJ: Ablex.

Bank, S., & Kahn, M. D. (1982). *The sibling bond*. New York: Basic Books.

Begun, A. (1995). Sibling relationships and foster care placements for young children. *Early Child Development and Care, 106,* 237–250.

Bigby, C. (1997). Parental substitutes? The role of siblings in the lives of older people with intellectual disability. *Journal of Gerontological Social Work, 29,* 3–21.

Brodoff, A. S. (1988). First person account: Schizophrenia through a sister's eyes—the burden of invisible baggage. *Schizophrenia Bulletin, 14,* 113–116.

Brody, G. H. (1998). Sibling relationship quality: Its causes and consequences. *Annual Review of Psychology, 49,* 1–24.

Brody, G. H., Stoneman, Z., McCoy, J. K., & Forehand, R. (1992). Contemporary and longitudinal associations of sibling conflict with family relationship assessments and family discussions about sibling problems. *Child Development, 63,* 391–400.

Buckley, S. (2007). Brothers and sisters and Down syndrome. *Down Syndrome: Research and Practice, 12,* 8.

Cherlin, A. J. (2005). *Public and private families*. New York: McGraw-Hill.

Christensen, A., & Margolin, G. (1988). Conflict and alliance in distressed and non-distressed families. In R. A. Hinde & J. Stevenson-Hinde (Eds.), *Relationships within families: Mutual influences* (pp. 263–282). Oxford: Clarendon Press.

Cicirelli, V. G. (1992). Siblings as caregivers in middle and old age. In J. E. Dwyer & R. T. Coward (Eds.), *Gender, families, and elder care* (pp. 84–101). Thousand Oaks, CA: Sage.

Coleman, M., Ganong, L., & Fine, M. (2001). Reinvestigating remarriage: Another decade of progress. In R. M. Milardo (Ed.), *Understanding families into the new millennium: A decade review* (pp. 507–526). Minneapolis: National Council on Family Relations.

Conger, K. J. (2008). Sibling relationships. In W. A. Darity Jr. (Ed.), *International Encyclopedia of the Social Sciences* (2nd ed., Vol. 7, pp. 505–507). Woodbridge, CT: Macmillan Reference.

Conger, K. J., Bryant, C. M., & Brennom, J. M. (2004). The changing nature of adolescent sibling relationships. In R. D. Conger, F. O. Lorenz, & K.A.S. Wickrama (Eds.), *Continuity and change in family relations: Theory, methods, and empirical findings* (pp. 319–344). Mahwah, NJ: Erlbaum.

Conger, K. J., & Little, W. M. (in press). Sibling relationships during the transition to adulthood. *Child Development Perspectives.*

Conger, R. D., & Conger, K. J. (1996). Sibling relationships. In R. L. Simons (Ed.), *Understanding differences between divorced and intact families: Stress, interaction, and child outcome* (pp. 104–121). Thousand Oaks, CA: Sage.

Conley, D. (2004). *The pecking order: Which siblings succeed and why*. New York: Pantheon Books.

Connidis, I. A. (2001). *Family ties and aging*. Thousand Oaks, CA: Sage.

Connidis, I. A., & Campbell, L. D. (1995). Closeness, confiding, and contact among siblings in middle and late adulthood. *Journal of Family Issues, 16,* 722–745.

Cox, M. J., & Paley, B. (1997). Families as systems. *Annual Review of Psychology, 48,* 243–267.

Davies, P., & Cummings, E. M. (1994). Marital conflict and child adjustment: An emotional security hypothesis. *Psychological Bulletin, 116,* 387–411.

Depp, C. (1983). Placing siblings together. *Children Today, 12*(2), 14–19.

Dunn, J. (2007). Siblings and socialization. In J. E. Grusec & P. D. Hastings (Eds.), *Handbook of socialization: Theory and research* (pp. 309–327). New York: Guilford Press.

Dykens, E. M. (2005). Happiness, well-being, and character strengths: Outcomes for families and siblings of persons with mental retardation. *Mental Retardation, 43,* 360–364.

Elder, G. H. Jr. (1998). Life course theory. In R. M. Lerner (Vol. Ed.), *Handbook of child psychology, Vol. 1. Theoretical models of human development* (5th ed., pp. 939–991). Hoboken, NJ: Wiley.

Erel, O., Margolin, G., & John, R. S. (1998). Observed sibling interaction: Links with marital conflict and the mother-child relationship. *Developmental Psychology, 34,* 288–298.

Gass, K., Jenkins, J., & Dunn, J. (2007). Are sibling relationships protective? A longitudinal study. *Journal of Child Psychology and Psychiatry, 48,* 167–175.

Gath, A. (1992). The brothers and sisters of mentally retarded children. In F. Boer & J. Dunn (Eds.), *Children's sibling relationships: Developmental and clinical issues* (pp. 101–108). Hillsdale, NJ: Erlbaum.

Goetting, A. (1986). The developmental tasks of siblingship over the life cycle. *Journal of Marriage and the Family, 48,* 703–714.

Gold, N. (1993). Depression and social adjustment in siblings of boys with autism. *Journal of Autism and Developmental Disorders, 23,* 147–163.

Gray, D. E. (1998). *Autism and the family: Problems, prospects, and coping with the disorder.* Springfield, IL: Charles C. Thomas.

Grossman, F. (1972). *Brothers and sisters of retarded children.* Syracuse, NY: Syracuse University Press.

Grych, J. H., & Fincham, F. D. (1990). Marital conflict and children's adjustment: A cognitive-contextual framework. *Psychological Bulletin, 108,* 267–290.

Harold, G. T., Fincham, F. D., Osborne, L. N., & Conger, R. D. (1997). Mom and Dad are at it again: Adolescent perceptions of marital conflict and adolescent psychological distress. *Developmental Psychology, 33,* 333–350.

Herrick, M. A., & Piccus, W. (2005). Sibling connections: The importance of nurturing sibling bonds in the foster care system. *Children and Youth Services Review, 27,* 845–861.

Hetherington, E. M. (1988). Parents, children, and siblings: Six years after divorce. In R. A. Hinde & J. Stevenson-Hinde (Eds.), *Relationships within families: Mutual influences* (pp. 311–331). Oxford: Clarendon Press.

Hodapp, R. M., Glidden, L. M., & Kaiser, A. P. (2005). Siblings of persons with disabilities: Toward a research agenda. *Mental Retardation, 43,* 334–338.

Howe, N., & Ross, H. S. (1990). Socialization, perspective taking, and the sibling relationship. *Developmental Psychology, 26,* 160–165.

Jenkins, J. (1992). Sibling relationships in disharmonious homes: Potential difficulties and protective effects. In F. Boer & J. Dunn (Eds.), *Children's sibling relationships: Developmental and clinical issues* (pp. 125–138). Hillsdale, NJ: Erlbaum.

Jenkins, J. M., Dunn, J., Rasbash, J., O'Connor, T. G., & Simpson, A. (2005). The mutual influence of marital conflict and children's behavior problems: Shared and non-shared family risks. *Child Development, 76,* 24–39.

Kaplan, L., Hennon, C. B., & Ade-Ridder, L. (1993). Splitting custody of children between parents: Impacts on the sibling system. *Families in Society: The Journal of Contemporary Human Services, 30,* 131–144.

Kempton, T., Armistead, L., Wierson, M., & Forehand, R. (1991). Presence of a sibling as a potential buffer following parental divorce: An examination of young adolescents. *Journal of Clinical Child Psychology, 20,* 434–438.

Kramer, L. (2004). Experimental interventions in sibling relations. In R. D. Conger, F. O. Lorenz, & K.A.S. Wickrama (Eds.), *Continuity and change in family relations: Theory, methods and empirical findings* (pp. 345–380). Mahwah, NJ: Erlbaum.

Leathers, S. J. (2005). Separation from siblings: Associations with placement adaptation and outcomes among adolescents in long-term foster care. *Children and Youth Services Review, 27,* 793–819.

Linares, L. O. (2006). An understudied form of intra-family violence: Sibling-to-sibling aggression among foster children. *Aggression and Violent Behavior, 11,* 95–109.

MacKinnon, C. E. (1989). An observational investigation of sibling interactions in married and divorced families. *Developmental Psychology, 25,* 36–44.

Macks, R. J., & Reeve, R. E. (2007). The adjustment of non-disabled siblings of children with autism. *Journal of Autism and Developmental Disorders, 37,* 1060–1067.

McGuire, S., & Shanahan, L. (in press). Sibling relationships in diverse family contexts. *Child Development Perspectives.*

NEW DIRECTIONS FOR CHILD AND ADOLESCENT DEVELOPMENT • DOI: 10.1002/cd

McHale, S. M., & Harris, V. S. (1992). Children's experiences with disabled and nondisabled siblings: Links with personal adjustment and relationship evaluations. In F. Boer & J. Dunn (Eds.), *Children's sibling relationships: Developmental and clinical issues* (pp. 83–100). Mahwah, NJ: Erlbaum.

Milevsky, A. (2004). Perceived parental marital satisfaction and divorce: Effects on sibling relations in emerging adulthood. *Journal of Divorce and Remarriage, 41,* 115–128.

Milevsky, A. (2005). Compensatory patterns of sibling support in emerging adulthood: Variations in loneliness, self-esteem, depression and life satisfaction. *Journal of Social and Personal Relationships, 22,* 743–755.

Morgan, S. B. (1988). The autistic child and family functioning: A developmental family systems perspective. *Journal of Autism and Developmental Disorders, 16,* 399–413.

Nuckolls, C. W. (Ed). (1993). *Siblings of South Asia: Brothers and sisters in cultural context.* New York: Guilford Press.

Panish, J. B., & Stricker, G. (2001). Parental marital conflict in childhood and influence on adult sibling relationships. *Journal of Psychotherapy in Independent Practice, 2,* 3–16.

Parke, R. D., & Buriel, R. (1998). Socialization in the family: Ethnic and ecological perspectives. In N. Eisenberg (Vol. Ed.), *Handbook of Child Psychology, Vol. 3. Social, emotional, and personality development* (5th ed., pp. 463–552). Hoboken, NJ: Wiley.

Patterson, G. R. (1986). The contribution of siblings to training for fighting: A microsocial analysis. In J. Block, D. Olweus, & M. Radke-Yarrow (Eds.), *Development of antisocial and prosocial behavior* (pp. 235–261). Orlando, FL: Academic Press.

Poortman, A., & Voorpostel, M. (2009). Parental divorce and sibling relationships: A research note. *Journal of Family Issues, 30,* 74–91.

Richmond, M. K., & Stocker, C. M. (2006). Associations between family cohesion and adolescent siblings' externalizing behavior. *Journal of Family Psychology, 20,* 663–669.

Riggio, H. R. (2001). Relations between parental divorce and the quality of adult sibling relationships. *Journal of Divorce and Remarriage, 36,* 67–82.

Rivers, J. W., & Stoneman, Z. (2003). Sibling relationships when a child has autism: Marital stress and support coping. *Journal of Autism and Developmental Disorders, 33,* 383–394.

Sakai, A., Sugawara, M., Maeshiro, K., Amou, Y. & Takuma, T. (2002). Negative life events in childhood and puberty: Role of children's trust in parents and siblings as protective factor of depression. *Journal of Mental Health, 48,* 71–83.

Schacter, F. F., & Stone, R. K. (1987). Comparing and contrasting siblings: Defining the self. In F. F. Schacter & R. K. Stone (Eds.), *Practical concerns about siblings: Bridging the research-practice gap* (pp. 55–76). New York: Haworth.

Seltzer, M. M., Greenberg, J. S., Orsmond, G. I., & Lounds, J. (2005). Life course studies of siblings of individuals with developmental disabilities. *Mental Retardation, 43,* 354–359.

Sharpe, D., & Rossiter, L. (2002). Siblings of children with a chronic illness: A meta-analysis. *Journal of Pediatric Psychology, 27,* 699–710.

Sheehan, G., Darlington, Y., Noller, P., & Feeney, J. (2004). Children's perceptions of their sibling relationships during parental separation and divorce. *Journal of Divorce and Remarriage, 41,* 69–94.

Shlonsky, A., Bellamy, J., Elkins, J., & Ashare, C. J. (2005). The other kin: Setting the course for research, policy, and practice with siblings in foster care. *Children and Youth Services Review, 27,* 697–716.

Simons, R. L., & Associates. (1996). *Understanding differences between divorced and intact families: Stress, interaction, and child outcome.* Thousand Oaks, CA: Sage.

Skopp, N. A., McDonald, R., Manke, B., & Jouriles, E. N. (2005). Siblings in domestically violent families: Experiences of interparent conflict and adjustment problems. *Journal of Family Psychology, 19,* 324–337.

Smith, M. C. (1998). Sibling placement in foster care: An exploration of associated concurrent preschool-aged child functioning. *Children and Youth Services Review, 20,* 389–412.

Stewart, R. (1983). Sibling interaction: The role of the older child as a teacher for the younger. *Merrill-Palmer Quarterly, 29,* 47–68.

Stocker, C., Ahmed, K., & Stall, M. (1997). Marital satisfaction and maternal emotional expressiveness: Links with children's siblings relationships. *Social Development, 63,* 373–385.

Stocker, C., & Youngblade, L. (1999). Marital conflict and parental hostility: Links with children's sibling and peer relationships. *Journal of Family Psychology, 13,* 598–609.

Stoneman, Z., & Berman, P. W. (Eds.). (1993). *The effects of mental retardation, disability and illness on sibling relationships: Research issues and challenges.* Baltimore, MD: Brooke.

Tarren-Sweeney, M., & Hazell, P. (2005). The mental health and socialization of siblings in care. *Children and Youth Services Review, 27,* 821–843.

Teti, D. M., & Ablard, K. E. (1989). Security of attachment and infant-sibling relationships: A laboratory study. *Child Development, 60,* 1519–1528.

U.S. Department of Health and Human Services. Administration of Children, Youth and Families. Children's Bureau. (2008). *Child maltreatment 2006.* Washington, DC: Government Printing Office.

Webster, D., Shlonsky, A., Shaw, T., & Brookhart, M. A. (2005). The ties that bind II: Reunification for siblings in out-of-home care using a statistical technique for examining non-independent observations. *Children and Youth Service Review, 27,* 765–783.

Weisner, T. S. (1989). Comparing sibling relationships across cultures. In P. Zukow-Goldring (Ed.), *Sibling interaction across cultures: Theoretical and cultural issues* (pp. 11–25). New York: Springer-Verlag.

Weisner, T. S. (1993). Overview: Sibling similarity and difference in different cultures. In C. W. Nuckolls (Ed.), *Siblings in South Asia: Brothers and sisters in cultural context* (pp. 1–17). New York: Guilford Press.

Zukow-Goldring, P. (2002). Sibling caregiving. In M. H. Bornstein (Ed.), *Handbook of parenting: Vol. 3. Being and becoming a parent* (pp. 253–286). Mahwah, NJ: Erlbaum.

KATHERINE J. CONGER is associate professor of human development in the Department of Human and Community Development at the University of California, Davis. E-mail: kjconger@ucdavis.edu.

CLARE STOCKER is associate research professor in the Department of Psychology at the University of Denver, Colorado. E-mail: cstocker@du.edu.

SHIRLEY MCGUIRE is professor of psychology and director of child and youth studies in the Department of Psychology at the University of San Francisco, California. E-mail: mcguire@usfca.edu.

NEW DIRECTIONS FOR CHILD AND ADOLESCENT DEVELOPMENT • DOI: 10.1002/cd

Stormshak, E. A., Bullock, B. M., & Falkenstein, C. A. (2009). Harnessing the power of sibling relationships as a tool for optimizing social–emotional development. In L. Kramer & K. J. Conger (Eds.), *Siblings as agents of socialization. New Directions for Child and Adolescent Development, 126*, 61–77. San Francisco: Jossey-Bass.

5

Harnessing the Power of Sibling Relationships as a Tool for Optimizing Social–Emotional Development

Elizabeth A. Stormshak, Bernadette M. Bullock,
Corrina A. Falkenstein

Abstract

Sibling relationships provide one of the most stable and powerful developmental contexts for the transmission of both prosocial and antisocial behavior. As a source of support and skill development, sibling relationships can build competence in self-regulation and emotional understanding. However, sibling relationships marked by antisocial behavior, substance use, and conflict place children at risk for a host of negative outcomes. Family relationship features, particularly parenting practices and discord, contribute strongly to both the quality of sibling relationships and children's well-being. Our review of intervention strategies reveals that the potential of sibling relationships to promote socioemotional development may be best realized through family-centered approaches that build prosocial sibling interactions, curtail child behavior problems, and strengthen parenting. © Wiley Periodicals, Inc.

The work described in this chapter was supported by grants DA11997 and DA018734 from the National Institutes of Health to Elizabeth Stormshak, as well as grants DA018760, DA07031, and DA16110, also from the National Institutes of Health.

61

Most people who grow up with one or more sisters or brothers know that sibling relationships can greatly influence the social climate of a family. Within the home, siblings typically function as models of a wide variety of behaviors that range from socially acceptable to unacceptable. In addition, siblings often serve as guides to the social world outside the reaches of family influence (Dunn, Brown, & Beardsall, 1991). This chapter provides an overview of the sibling outcome literature from an ecological perspective. As we review research findings that highlight the positive aspects of sibling relationships that can be harnessed to optimize youth development, we also explore the potentially negative impact of sibling relationships, particularly, deviancy training, collusion, and coercive relationship patterns. We conclude with a brief presentation of our model of a family-centered intervention that addresses youth problem behaviors.

Although social development research has long focused on parent-child relationship processes within the family and for the most part has neglected sibling relationship dynamics, this focus has changed during the past several decades. Systemic views of parenting now acknowledge that parenting does not occur in a vacuum and that the sibling subsystem provides a unique and powerful influence that can promote, detract, or be independent from parents' efforts to socialize their children (for reviews, see Brody, 1998; Volling, 2003). It is clear that the quality of sibling relationship can predict longitudinal adjustment from middle childhood well into adolescence (Bank, Burraston, & Snyder, 2004; Kim, McHale, Crouter, & Osgood, 2007).

An Ecological Approach to Understanding Sibling Adjustment

The quality of the sibling relationship can profoundly affect children's socioemotional development, with both positive and negative outcomes. Figure 5.1 presents an ecological model for understanding child adjustment as a function of the social processes that children experience within family and societal contexts. The family context may include both risk factors and strengths, some of which are shown in the figure. Risk factors such as marital problems, depression, substance use, and experiences of discrimination undermine parenting and place youth at risk for later problem behavior. Protective factors such as healthy marital relationships, low stress, and clear family values support family management skills and positive youth adjustment. Because sibling relationships occur in the context of families, they are vulnerable to the risk and protective factors that are directly related to parenting and youth problem behavior. A dynamic interaction between family management and sibling adaptation mediates the link between contextual risk factors and later child adjustment and is shaped by the family's culture and values. This developmental model organizes our discussion of siblings and the literature that supports the links between sibling adjustment and social-emotional development across childhood.

NEW DIRECTIONS FOR CHILD AND ADOLESCENT DEVELOPMENT • DOI: 10.1002/cd

Figure 5.1. Ecological Model of Family Social Processes Related to Child Adjustment

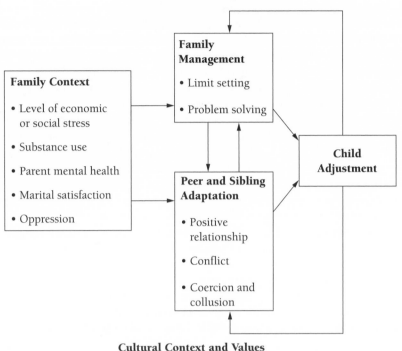

Cultural Context and Values

Positive Sibling Relationships and Social Development

Most children spend more time interacting with their siblings than with parents, and children are involved with their siblings every day in multiple ways (Dunn, 1983; McHale & Crouter, 1996). A recent study of sibling quality and time revealed that siblings spend an average of ten hours together per week in both constructive and unstructured activities (Tucker, McHale, & Crouter, 2008). As children enter adolescence, they experience less conflict with their siblings and increased gender-based differences in support and intimacy (Kim, McHale, Osgood, & Crouter, 2006). Same-sex girl dyads remain stable in their support and intimacy, whereas boy dyads decrease in intimacy and support as adolescents. The amount of time siblings spend together in constructive activities predicts self-esteem for both older and younger siblings and peer competence for younger siblings, particularly for girls (Tucker et al., 2008). Not surprisingly, sibling relationships provide one of the most stable and powerful developmental contexts for the transmission of both antisocial and prosocial behavior.

NEW DIRECTIONS FOR CHILD AND ADOLESCENT DEVELOPMENT • DOI: 10.1002/cd

Self-Regulation. One factor related to the development of both externalizing and internalizing behavior is self-regulation: the ability to regulate behavior during stressful situations, maintain focused attention, and modulate underlying reactivity (Rothbart & Derryberry, 1981). Self-regulation is also related to constructs such as effortful control (Rothbart & Rueda, 2005) and emotional regulation (Blair, Denham, Kochanoff, & Whipple, 2004). Given the nature of the sibling relationship, it seems logical that self-regulation skills would develop in the context of positive sibling relationships. This model is consistent with much of the early work on sibling relationships that focused on feeling state language development, perspective taking, and affective control (Brown & Dunn, 1992; Dunn et al., 1991; Howe, 1991). Nonetheless, we know little about the linkages between self-regulation in the context of the sibling relationship and later positive adjustment.

Brody, Stoneman, Smith, and Gibson (1999) tested a model in which family relationships and parent psychological resources predict child self-regulation, which in turn predicts the quality of the sibling relationship. They found that in a sample of eighty-five African American youth, the links between family processes and sibling relationship quality were fully mediated by self-regulation. This research was not longitudinal, and so the directionality of effects is unclear. Does self-regulation predict sibling relationship quality, or is the reverse true? Either way, positive sibling relationships are related to a child's ability to self-regulate emotions and develop social competence. Even after controlling for children's relationships with parents, positive sibling relationships in middle childhood predict youth adjustment (Pike, Coldwell, & Dunn, 2005). It is clear that positive sibling relationships in the context of a supportive family environment can have positive benefits for youth, including reducing the risk of later depression and enhancing social competence with peers (Kim et al., 2007; Stormshak, Bellanti, & Bierman, 1996).

Parenting Practices. Parenting practices have long been known to directly affect the quality of sibling relationships. Factors such as harsh, inconsistent, or differential parenting, in which one sibling is treated with more positivity or negativity than another, have consistently been found to affect both the quality of the sibling relationship and behavioral outcomes (McHale, Updegraff, Jackson-Newson, Tucker, & Crouter, 2000; Brody, Stoneman, & McCoy, 1992). Children who are exposed to harsh parenting and environments characterized by unresolved disputes are significantly more likely to develop a behavioral repertoire that fosters conflictual interactions with siblings. In particular, they are more likely to handle disputes by means of aggressive, coercive behaviors, interpret neutral sibling interactions as hostile or aggressive, or be motivated by negative, self-serving intentions (Brody, Arias, & Fincham, 1996; Crick & Dodge, 1994; Fincham, 1994).

Differential parenting, or children's perceptions that one sibling is being treated more favorably than another, also affects the quality of the sibling relationship and later child adjustment. When children perceive fairness in the parenting system, sibling relationships are more positive and are linked to better adjustment (Kowal, Kramer, Krull, & Crick, 2002; McHale et al., 2000). Similarly, differential parenting creates stress in the marital dyad and has been linked to longitudinal changes in marital quality from the offsprings' middle childhood to adolescence (Kan, McHale, & Crouter, 2008). A variety of studies on family dynamics have shown that behaviors during dyadic disagreements, and sibling perceptions of parental behavior during such encounters, have significant bearing on child development (Feinberg, Neiderhiser, Simmens, Reiss, & Hetherington, 2000; McGuire, Manke, Eftekhari, & Dunn, 2000; McHale et al., 2000; Vuchinich, Emery, & Cassidy, 1988).

Siblings: Fellow Travelers on the Developmental Road

More than twenty years ago, Gerald Patterson published "Siblings: Fellow Travelers in Coercive Family Processes" (Patterson, 1984), an important chapter about the role of parent attention, effort, and skill in the management of sibling dynamics. Early research on the coercive model suggested that antisocial siblings are involved in high levels of conflict and engage in more coercive interactions in the home than target children engage in with their parents (Loeber & Tengs, 1986). In the decades that followed, researchers discovered that siblings are fellow travelers on an expansive developmental path that includes both antisocial and prosocial outcomes (Abramovitch, Corter, & Lando, 1979; Rowe, 1981; Scarr & Grajek, 1982). For example, chronic conflict and coercion between siblings have been linked to academic difficulty, poor peer relations (Abramovitch et al., 1979; Rowe, 1981; Scarr & Grajek, 1982), the development and maintenance of aggressive behavior (Bank, Patterson, & Reid, 1996), adolescent substance abuse, and pervasive feelings of inadequacy, incompetence, and hostility in young adulthood (Bank et al., 1996; Dunn, Slomkowski, Beardsall, & Rende, 1984). Conversely, positive sibling relationships have been found to promote the development of prosocial behavior (Patterson, 1984), including empathy, social skills, and academic competence, as well as provide emotional support (Stormshak et al., 1996; Tucker, Updegraff, McHale, & Crouter, 1999). Close sibling relationships in adolescence may protect youth from the development of depression and may support positive adjustment, particularly among girls (Kim et al., 2007; McHale, Crouter, & Tucker, 1999).

Although a substantial literature describes the influence of sibling relationships across various domains of development, these studies have generated inconsistent results. For example, some studies revealed that the association between sibling support and developmental outcomes yielded negative correlations between older sibling support and younger sibling adjustment even after controlling for gender, race, family activities, and the perception of the family environment (Widmer & Weiss, 2000). One might assume these results suggest that a supportive relationship with an older sibling is associated with poorer adjustment for younger siblings. In contrast, warmth in sibling relationships has been associated with fewer conduct problems and reports of loneliness, and greater self-worth (East & Rook, 1992; Kim et al., 2007; Stocker, 1994). In addition, warmth and positive sibling relations that occur in the context of deviant behavior and coercion have a negative impact on later youth adjustment and predict problem behavior for both siblings (Slomkowski, Rende, Conger, Simons, & Conger, 2001; Stormshak, Comeau, & Shepard, 2004).

The complex picture that emerges from this research is that because sibling relationships occur in the context of families, they cannot be disentangled from the relationships that children have with their parents and peers or from the role that parenting skills play in sibling outcomes. At the same time, many factors in a child's environment simultaneously influence both sibling relationship and developmental outcomes.

It is likely, given the model presented in Figure 5.1, that factors such as child temperament (Brody, Stoneman, & Gauger, 1996; Stoneman & Brody, 1993), age gap and gender differences (Brownfield & Sorenson, 1994), absence of identification with siblings (Schachter & Stone, 1985), level of parental involvement in sibling conflict (McHale, Updegraff, Jackson-Newson, Tucker, & Crouter, 2000), child perceptions of differential parental treatment (Feinberg et al., 2000; Kowal & Kramer, 1997; McHale et al., 2000), and cultural context (McHale, Whiteman, Kim, & Crouter, 2007) contribute to the inconsistency of these findings. Each of these family and contextual influences may differentially affect the nature of the sibling relationship and behavioral outcomes.

Relationship Processes: Coercion and Collusion in the Sibling Relationship

Although several studies provide evidence that older siblings may influence the initiation of their younger siblings' substance use or delinquency (Brook, Whiteman, Gordon, & Brenden, 1983; Conger & Rueter, 1996; Duncan, Duncan, & Hops, 1996), the mechanisms underlying such influence are poorly understood. Siblings may share a history of coercive interactions with parents that set them on a trajectory toward poor academic performance and deviant peer relations. This coercive family history may lead children with antisocial characteristics to function as "trainers" of antisocial behavior for their siblings (Loeber & Tengs, 1986; Patterson, 1982, 1984). As children in the same family mutually develop patterns of problem behavior, it is possible that they actively form coalitions of deviance both within the family and outside the home in shared peer networks (Bullock & Dishion, 2002).

Two relationship processes have been directly associated with child and adolescent behavior problems: coercion and collusion. *Coercion* refers to a process by which siblings use aggression and other aversive behaviors to terminate conflict. *Collusion* refers to a mechanism by which siblings reinforce deviant behavior through the positive reinforcement of rule-breaking talk.

Coercion. The coercion model of antisocial behavior posits that problem behavior is the product of an interactive process in which family members encourage antisocial acts through repetitive negative reinforcement sequences (Patterson, 1982). Children with an antisocial sibling have been found to be both affected by the behavior of this sibling and influential in shaping the behavior of this sibling in the course of coercive exchanges in the home (Patterson, 1984). Siblings in distressed families have been reported to be more coercive than those in nondistressed families and more likely to extend a coercive sequence in the event of an antisocial sibling's attack. Because siblings in troubled families are participants in a distressed system that is influenced by the contribution of all family members, coercive sibling interactions are fundamental determinants for future antisocial conduct, with siblings functioning as teachers and pupils (Patterson, 1984, 1986).

Coercive sibling relationships are predictive of later adjustment difficulties for boys with identified behavior problems, as well as for their siblings. Negative patterns of sibling interaction during middle childhood have been found to be not only prognostic of future maladjustment, but also to be among the best predictors of boys' psychopathology in adolescence and early adulthood (Bank et al., 1996). Synchronous negative interactions with mothers and siblings during middle childhood have consistently predicted adult arrests and severity of criminal history, particularly for boys.

In families engaged in high rates of conflict and coercion, sibling interaction may be simply another context in which children learn to use aggression and other forms of aversive behaviors. Parents who do not attend to and manage sibling play may be inadvertently allowing conflicts to be resolved by means of coercion. Coercion, then, is a process embedded in family conflict and negative affect and is highly related to contentious sibling relationships and concurrent and future antisocial behavior (Bank et al., 1996).

Collusion. Although coercion emphasizes the relative contribution of negative sibling dynamics to conduct problems, recent observational research suggests that positive interactions among siblings may also lead to the development of a maladaptive behavioral repertoire (Bullock & Dishion, 2002; Criss & Shaw, 2005). Sibling collusion is a process by which siblings form coalitions that promote deviance and undermine parenting. Videotaped family interactions have revealed a process by which siblings in families with a child at high risk for conduct problems exhibit reliably higher rates of collusion than do those in families with a normative target child. Sibling collusion also accounts for variance in problem behavior, including delinquency and substance use, after controlling for involvement with deviant peers (Bullock & Dishion, 2002). Collusive attempts to undermine parental efforts to monitor and set limits regarding behavior form a common ground among siblings, potentially amplifying the risk of mutuality in problem behavior

NEW DIRECTIONS FOR CHILD AND ADOLESCENT DEVELOPMENT • DOI: 10.1002/cd

during early adolescence. This process is found to persist one year later, suggesting that this dynamic may be relatively stable during adolescence (Bullock & Dishion, 2001).

Siblings and Substance Use. Ample research supports the links between siblings and substance use. As discussed by Whiteman, Becerra, and Killoren in Chapter Three in this volume, younger siblings are exposed to substances and often initiate use at an earlier age than older siblings do (Bank et al., 1996; Brook, Whiteman, Gordon, & Brenden, 1983). We examined the links between siblings' substance use and youth access to substances over time by videotaping sibling interaction and learning about youth, sibling, and family dynamics in 161 families enrolled in our Project Alliance study. We measured substance use, antisocial behavior, and peer deviance over time, through age nineteen. We found that sibling deviance in sixth grade predicted siblings' increased substance use over time, with higher levels of sibling deviance predicting greater growth in substance use (see Figure 5.2). Using lag sequential modeling, we observed that initial levels of sibling deviance in sixth grade predicted the degree of both seventh-grade substance use and siblings' use and access to substances. Access to substances through sibling use continued to significantly predict the use of substances for our target youth through age nineteen. Sibling substance use and access to substances through siblings predict 27 percent of the variance in target child substance use by age nineteen (see Figure 5.3). Clearly sibling substance use and access to substances through siblings is a major contributor to youths' later problem behavior.

Figure 5.2. Growth of Substance Use Predicted by Sibling Deviance over Time

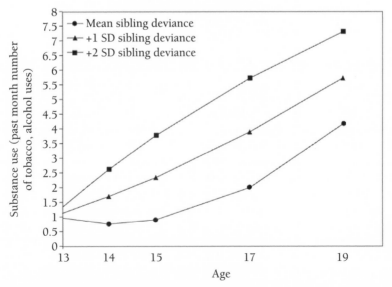

Figure 5.3. Longitudinal Influences of Sibling Behavior on Substance Use

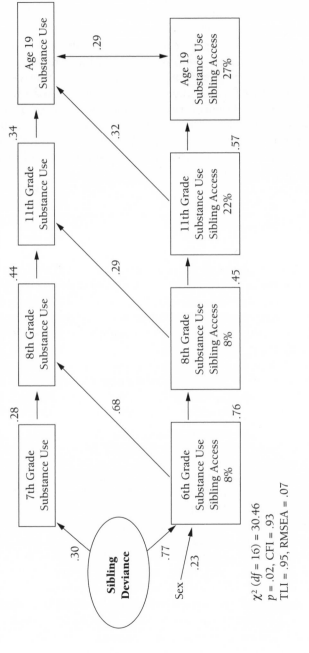

Clearly sibling relationships are influenced by multiple factors. They are sensitive to contextual risks and protective factors such as parents' marital quality, parenting skills and behaviors, and adult mental health; these family context factors may have both immediate and long-term effects on individual adjustment. That said, our attention must turn to effective interventions with siblings and a model for intervention with siblings and families. The literature has demonstrated the salient role siblings play in the development of various problem behaviors and positive outcomes and provides support for the importance of family-based interventions that target the sibling relationship as a mechanism of change (Rowe, Rodgers, & Meseck-Bushey, 1992). Accordingly, a family-centered, ecologically based treatment model that includes the targeted child and the people and contexts that are meaningful to the child, including siblings, is most likely to promote positive youth outcomes.

A Family-Centered Approach to Working with Problem Behavior

As this review suggests, siblings can profoundly affect child development through coercive and collusive relationship patterns that may contribute to problem behaviors, such as substance use and delinquency. On the basis of the research described in this chapter, it is logical to assume that working directly with siblings, or with siblings and parents, may reduce these problems. Interestingly, very few intervention studies focus exclusively on the sibling relationship. This is primarily because for many families, increasing communication and interaction between high-risk siblings may actually increase problem behavior among younger siblings if they are exposed to high-risk behavior. Our research suggests that in some cases, reducing exposure to high-risk siblings may be the best treatment strategy for younger siblings and other vulnerable family members. Interventions aimed at improving parenting skills such as monitoring, positive reinforcement, and appropriate limit setting often trickle down to influence the nature of the sibling relationship and sibling developmental outcomes. Overall, a targeted approach to family intervention that builds on the ecological model and considers the context of development for the family and each child is warranted.

We use a multilevel model for engaging and intervening with families that explicitly integrates intervention targets, such as family management, parent-child relationships, and sibling relationships, with principles of behavior change (Dishion & Kavanagh, 2003; Dishion & Stormshak, 2007). In this model, called EcoFIT, we tailor interventions with children and families to fit their current family circumstances on the basis of the assessment results of the Family Check-Up (FCU). The FCU provides an ecological assessment that addresses parents' motivation to change (see Miller & Rollnick, 2002). We videotape family interactions and collect data from parents, teachers, and youth involved in the intervention. We then provide feedback to families using motivational interviewing techniques that are strengths based and adapted for each family's needs.

Some families may participate in interventions that target only the encouragement of skills, such as positive reinforcement, especially if limit setting, parental monitoring, and communication are found through the assessment to be parenting strengths. Or we may tailor our approach to building limit setting, depending on the number of parents in the family, qualities of the sibling dyad and behavior of individual siblings, and families' sociocultural background. In this sense, the EcoFIT approach proposes a menu of empirically supported interventions with diverse venues of service delivery. Offering an intervention menu and a variety of flexible service delivery options promotes parent engagement and motivation (Dishion & Kavanagh, 2003; Miller & Rollnick, 2002).

This approach to intervention reduces the focus on one particular target child while increasing the focus on family management, siblings, and contexts of change (see Figure 5.1). As such, the treatment may vary depending on the particular circumstances of the child and sibling. For example, in a family in which an older sibling uses drugs and spends a lot of time alone with a younger sibling, the intervention may focus on altering the children's schedules and increasing parental supervision of both children after school. For families involved in coercive relationship patterns and those in which sibling collusion is undermining parents' authority in the home, interventions may be tailored to improve parents' ability to extinguish the coercive cycle, improve family relationship quality, and reduce siblings' ability to negatively influence family dynamics. Alternatively, in a family where siblings are close and mutually supportive with low rates of problem behavior, the intervention may include activities with siblings that support teamwork and a positive sibling relationship, as well as encouragement and incentives to support effective parenting. This approach enables all family members to benefit when a child is referred for treatment.

Our intervention model parallels recent research focused directly on parenting and the effects of parenting interventions on multiple siblings. Brotman and colleagues (Brotman et al., 2005; Brotman, Gouley, O'Neal, & Klein, 2004) found that parents with an adolescent engaged in serious delinquent behaviors were motivated to participate in a program focused on preventing problem behaviors in their younger preschool-age children (Brotman et al., 2003, 2004). Most striking, they found that their intervention that strengthened the parenting of preschool children also improved older adolescent siblings' peer relationships and reduced antisocial behavior even though most of these adolescents did not directly participate in the intervention. These results suggest that interventions with parents and young siblings can improve parenting practices that generalize to produce fewer problem behaviors of older adolescent siblings.

Brestan, Eyberg, Boggs, and Algina (1997) also tested the generalizability of treatment effects on nontargeted siblings. Parents and children referred for conduct problems engaged in parent–child interaction training, and the investigators examined the effects of the training on the siblings not involved in treatment. Treatment focused on addressing the referred child's behavior, and parents were encouraged not to include siblings in home practice skills. When compared with the control group, both untreated siblings and the referred children were reported by parents to exhibit fewer conduct problems. This study further supports the notion that treating one child may have spillover effects on siblings who are residing in the home, even when these siblings are not directly involved in treatment.

Kennedy and Kramer (2008) developed a preventive intervention designed to help siblings aged four to eight years improve their sibling relationship by developing emotional competencies and prosocial behaviors. Results suggest that sibling relationships are amenable to intervention and that teaching emotion regulation skills to siblings may be a key domain for improving sibling relationship quality. This outcome is important for understanding the developmental context in which sibling relationships operate.

Although we have not directly tested the impact of the FCU on sibling interactions, we have examined whether this intervention improves basic parenting skills, such as monitoring children and providing support. The model has been applied in both early childhood and adolescence. In the Early Steps project, young children starting at age two were the primary focus of the intervention. The FCU intervention significantly improved both problem behavior and observed positive behavior support of parents, as well as proactive parenting (Dishion et al., 2008; Gardner, Shaw, Dishion, Burton, & Supplee, 2007). Improving parenting skills with one child will likely have the benefit of improved parenting with all children in the family. Relationships with family members are dynamic processes that change and influence development over time (Dishion & Snyder, 2004). The improvement of any relationship in the family would likely have a positive impact on the relationships of other family members. The effects of the EcoFIT intervention on sibling relationship quality can be examined in future research.

Conclusion

It is surprising that so little consideration has been given to the role of siblings in child and family treatment considering the longevity of the sibling relationship and the role of siblings in the development of positive and negative youth behaviors. The studies described in this chapter support the notion that the role of siblings in family relationships and treatment outcomes is complex and that it warrants increased attention in both clinical and research domains. Mechanisms of sibling socialization should be considered when developing larger intervention studies and family-centered approaches to treatment. As portrayed in the ecological model presented in Figure 5.1, sibling relationships do not exist in isolation; rather, they are significantly shaped by family relationships within the larger sociocultural context.

Sibling relationships are key predictors of youth outcomes, affecting both positive adjustment and problem behaviors. It would be desirable to state that sibling relationships characterized by positive support and intimacy predict enhanced developmental outcomes, whereas those characterized by negative interactions and conflict predict poor outcomes. Yet the picture that emerges from the sibling literature is much more complex, suggesting that additional factors, such as parenting, self-regulation, and peer relationships, also play a role in mutually influencing sibling relationships and subsequent outcomes. Interaction effects are likely; for example, some positive sibling interaction processes (such as support) may be detrimental when they occur in the context of deviant behavior (substance use, for example). Alternatively, some negative sibling interaction processes, such as conflict, can paradoxically have a positive influence on development because they contribute to the acquisition of social skills and conflict negotiation. Intervention models that take these complexities into consideration and target potential mediating factors, such as family, peer, and sibling relationship processes, will be most successful at reducing later risk for youth.

Future intervention models should strive to integrate these research findings to identify effective intervention strategies that reduce risk and promote positive adjustment over time. Clearly interventions that boost the positive aspects of the sibling relationship while addressing potential negative influences are promising interventions for at-risk youth. These interventions should occur in the context of family-based models that reduce contextual risks while promoting protective factors and environmental supports. Intervention models that directly test the impact of family-centered approaches on all siblings will be vital to furthering our understanding of effective treatments for youth.

References

Abramovitch, R., Corter, C., & Lando, B. (1979). Sibling interaction in the home. *Child Development, 50*, 997–1003.

Bank, L., Burraston, B., & Snyder, J. (2004). Sibling conflict and ineffective parenting as predictors of adolescent boys' antisocial behavior and peer difficulties: Additive and interactional effects. *Journal of Research on Adolescence, 14*, 99–125.

Bank, L., Patterson, G. R., & Reid, J. B. (1996). Negative sibling interaction patterns as predictors of later adjustment problems in adolescent and young adult males. In G. H. Brody (Ed.), *Sibling relationships: Their causes and consequences* (pp. 197–229). Norwood, NJ: Ablex.

Blair, K. A., Denham, S. A., Kochanoff, A., & Whipple, B. (2004). Playing it cool: Temperament, emotional regulation, and social behavior in preschoolers. *Journal of School Psychology, 42*, 419–443.

Brestan, E. V., Eyberg, S. M., Boggs, S. R., & Algina, J. (1997). Parent–child interaction therapy: Parents' perceptions of untreated siblings. *Child and Family Behavior Therapy, 19*, 13–28.

Brody, G. H. (1998). Sibling relationship quality: Its causes and consequences. *Annual Review of Psychology, 49,* 1–24.

Brody, G. H., Arias, I., & Fincham, F. D. (1996). Linking marital and child attributions to family processes and parent–child relationships. *Journal of Family Psychology, 10,* 408–421.

Brody, G. H., Stoneman, Z., & Gauger, K. (1996). Parent–child relationships, family problem-solving behavior, and sibling relationship quality: The moderating role of sibling temperaments. *Child Development, 67,* 1289–1300.

Brody, G. H., Stoneman, Z., & McCoy, J. K. (1992). Parental differential treatment of siblings and sibling differences in negative emotionality. *Journal of Marriage and the Family, 54,* 643–651.

Brody, G. H., Stoneman, Z., Smith, T., & Gibson, N. (1999). Sibling relationships in rural African American families. *Journal of Marriage and the Family, 61,* 1046–1057.

Brook, J. S., Whiteman, M., Gordon, A. S., & Brenden, C. (1983). Older brother's influence on young sibling's drug use. *Journal of Psychology, 114,* 83–90.

Brotman, L. M., Gouley, K. K., Chesir-Teran, D., Dennis, T., Klein, R. G., & Shrout, P. (2005). Prevention for preschoolers at high risk for conduct problems: Immediate outcomes on parenting practices and child social competence. *Journal of Clinical and Adolescent Psychology, 34,* 724–734.

Brotman, L. M., Gouley, K. K., O'Neal, C., & Klein, R. G. (2004). Preschool-aged siblings of adjudicated youths: Multiple risk factors for conduct problems. *Early Education and Development, 15,* 387–406.

Brotman, L. M., Klein, R. G., Kamboukos, D., Brown, E. J., Coard, S. I., & Sosinsky, L. S. (2003). Preventive intervention for urban, low-income preschoolers at familial risk for conduct problems: A randomized pilot study. *Journal of Clinical Child and Adolescent Psychology, 32,* 246–257.

Brown, J. R., & Dunn, J. (1992). Talk with your mother or your sibling? Developmental changes in early family conversations about feelings. *Child Development, 63,* 336–349.

Brownfield, D., & Sorenson, A. M. (1994). Sibship size and sibling delinquency. *Deviant Behavior, 15,* 45–61.

Bullock, B. M., & Dishion, T. J. (2001, April). Sibling collusion, parenting and peers: Toward unraveling a multidirectional process. In E. A. Stormshak & B. M. Bullock (Chairs), *Sibling relationships as a context for the development of risk.* Paper presented at the biennial meeting of the Society for Research in Child Development, Minneapolis, MN.

Bullock, B. M., & Dishion, T. J. (2002). Sibling collusion and problem behavior in early adolescence: Towards a process model for family mutuality. *Journal of Abnormal Child Psychology, 30,* 143–153.

Conger, R. D., & Rueter, M. A. (1996). Siblings, parents and peers: A longitudinal study of social influence in adolescents at risk for alcohol use and abuse. In G. H. Brody (Ed.), *Sibling relationships: Their causes and consequences* (pp. 1–30). Norwood, NJ: Ablex.

Crick, N. R., & Dodge, K. A. (1994). A review and reformulation of social information processing mechanisms in children's social adjustment. *Psychological Bulletin, 115,* 74–101.

Criss, M. M., & Shaw, D. S. (2005). Sibling relationships as contexts for delinquency training in low-income families. *Journal of Family Psychology, 19,* 592–600.

Dishion, T. J., & Kavanagh, K. (2003). *Intervening in adolescent problem behavior: A family-centered approach.* New York: Guilford Press.

Dishion, T. J., Shaw, D. S., Connell, A. M., Gardner, F., Weaver, C. M., & Wilson, M. N. (2008). The Family Check-Up with high-risk indigent families: Preventing problem behavior by increasing parents' positive behavior support in early childhood. *Child Development, 79,* 1395–1414.

Dishion, T. J., & Snyder, J. (2004). An introduction to the special issue on advances in process and dynamic system analysis of social interaction and the development of anti-social behavior. *Journal of Abnormal Child Psychology, 32*, 575–578.

Dishion, T. J., & Stormshak, E. A. (2007). *Intervening in children's lives: An ecological, family-centered approach to mental health care.* Washington, DC: APA Books.

Duncan, T. E., Duncan, S. C., & Hops, H. (1996). The role of parents and older siblings in predicting adolescent substance use: Modeling development via structural equation latent growth methodology. *Journal of Family Psychology, 10*, 158–172.

Dunn, J. (1983). Sibling relationships in early childhood. *Child Development, 54*, 787–811.

Dunn, J., Brown, J., & Beardsall, L. (1991). Family talk about feeling states and children's later understanding of others' emotions. *Developmental Psychology, 27*, 448–455.

Dunn, J., Slomkowski, C., Beardsall, L., & Rende, R. (1994). Adjustment in middle childhood and early adolescence: Links with earlier and contemporary sibling relationships. *Journal of Child Psychology and Psychiatry, 35*, 491–504.

East, P. L., & Rook, K. S. (1992). Compensatory patterns of support among children's peer relationships: A test using friends, nonschool friends and siblings. *Developmental Psychology, 21*, 1016–1024.

Feinberg, M. E., Neiderhiser, J. M., Simmens, S., Reiss, D., & Hetherington, E. M. (2000). Sibling comparison of differential parental treatment in adolescence: Gender, self-esteem, and emotionality as mediators of the parenting-adjustment association. *Child Development, 71*, 1611–1628.

Fincham, F. D. (1994). Cognitions in marriage: Current status and future challenges. *Applied Prevention Psychology, 3*, 185–198.

Gardner, F., Shaw, D., Dishion, T. J., Burton, J., & Supplee, L. (2007). Randomized prevention trial for early conduct problems: Effects on proactive parenting and links to toddler disruptive behavior. *Journal of Family Psychology, 21*, 398–406.

Howe, N. (1991). Sibling directed internal state language, perspective-taking, and affective behavior. *Child Development, 62*, 1503–1512.

Kan, M. L., McHale, S. M., & Crouter, A. C. (2008). Interparental incongruence in differential treatment of adolescent siblings: Links with marital quality. *Journal of Marriage and Family, 70*, 466–479.

Kennedy, D. E., & Kramer, L. (2008). Improving emotion regulation and sibling relationship quality: The More Fun with Sisters and Brothers Program. *Family Relations, 57*, 567–578.

Kim, J.-Y., McHale, S. M., Crouter, A. C., & Osgood, D. W. (2007). Longitudinal linkages between sibling relationships and adjustment from middle childhood through adolescence. *Developmental Psychology, 43*, 960–973.

Kim, J.-Y., McHale, S. M., Osgood, D. W., & Crouter, A. C. (2006). Longitudinal course and family correlates of sibling relationships from childhood through adolescence. *Child Development, 77*, 1746–1761.

Kowal, A., & Kramer, L. (1997). Children's understanding of parental differential treatment. *Child Development, 68*, 113–126.

Kowal, A., Kramer, L., Krull, J. L., & Crick, N. (2002). Children's perceptions of the fairness of parental preferential treatment and their socioemotional well-being. *Journal of Family Psychology, 16*, 297–306.

Loeber, R., & Tengs, T. (1986). The analysis of coercive chains between children, mothers, and siblings. *Journal of Family Violence, 1*, 51–70.

McGuire, S., Manke, B., Eftekhari, A., & Dunn, J. (2000). Children's perceptions of sibling conflict during middle childhood: Issues and sibling (dis)similarity. *Social Development, 9*, 173–190.

McHale, S. M., & Crouter, A. C. (1996). The family contexts of children's sibling relationships. In G. H. Brody (Ed.), *Sibling relationships: Their causes and consequences* (pp. 173–195). Norwood, NJ: Ablex Publishing.

McHale, S. M., Crouter, A. C., & Tucker, C. J. (1999). Family context and gender role socialization in middle childhood: Comparing girls to boys and sisters to brothers. *Child Development, 70*, 990–1004.

McHale, S. M., Updegraff, K. A., Jackson-Newson, J., Tucker, C. J., & Crouter, A. C. (2000). When does parents' differential treatment have negative implications for siblings? *Social Development, 9*, 149–172.

McHale, S. M., Whiteman, S. D., Kim, J.-Y., & Crouter, A. C. (2007). Characteristics and correlates of sibling relationships in two-parent African American families. *Journal of Family Psychology, 21*, 227–235.

Miller, W. R., & Rollnick, S. (2002). *Motivational interviewing: Preparing people for change* (2nd ed.). New York: Guilford Press.

Patterson, G. R. (1982). *A social learning approach: III. Coercive family process.* Eugene, OR: Castalia.

Patterson, G. R. (1984). Siblings: Fellow travelers in coercive family processes. In R. J. Blanchard & D. C. Blanchard (Eds.), *Advances in the study of aggression* (Vol. 1, pp. 173–215). Orlando, FL: Academic Press.

Patterson, G. R. (1986). The contribution of siblings to training for fighting: A microsocial analysis. In D. Olweus, J. Block, & M. Radke-Yarrow (Eds.), *Development of antisocial and prosocial behaviors* (pp. 235–261). Orlando, FL: Academic Press.

Pike, A., Coldwell, J., & Dunn, J. F. (2005). Sibling relationships in early/middle childhood: Links with individual adjustment. *Journal of Family Psychology, 19*, 523–532.

Rothbart, M. K., & Derryberry, D. (1981). Development of individual differences in temperament. In M. E. Lamb & A. L Brown (Eds.), *Advances in developmental psychology* (Vol. 1, pp. 37–86). Mahwah, NJ: Erlbaum.

Rothbart, M. K., & Rueda, M.R. (2005). The development of effortful control. In U. Mayr, E. Awh, & S. Keele (Eds.), *Development individuality in the human brain: A tribute to Michael I. Posner* (pp. 167–188). Washington, DC: American Psychological Association.

Rowe, D. C. (1981). Environmental and genetic influences on dimensions of perceived parenting: A twin study. *Developmental Psychology, 17*, 203–208.

Rowe, D. C., Rodgers, J. L., & Meseck-Bushey, S. (1992). Sibling delinquency and the family environment: Shared and unshared influences. *Child Development, 63*, 59–67.

Scarr, S., & Grajek, S. (1982). Similarities and differences among siblings. In M. E. Lamb & B. Sutton-Smith (Eds.), *Sibling relationships: Their nature and significance across the lifespan* (pp. 357–381). Hillsdale, NJ: Erlbaum.

Schachter, F. F., & Stone, R. K. (1985). Pediatricians' and psychologists' implicit personality theory: Significance of sibling differences. *Journal of Developmental and Behavioral Pediatrics, 6*, 295–297.

Slomkowski, C., Rende, R., Conger, K. J., Simons, R. L., & Conger, R. D. (2001). Sisters, brothers, and delinquency: Evaluating social influence during early and middle adolescence. *Child Development, 72*, 271–283.

Stocker, C. M. (1994). Children's perceptions of relationships with siblings, friends, and mothers: Compensatory processes and links with adjustment. *Journal of Child Psychology and Psychiatry, 35*, 1447–1459.

Stoneman, Z., & Brody, G. H. (1993). Sibling temperaments, conflict, warmth, and role asymmetry. *Child Development, 64*, 1786–1800.

Stormshak, E. A., Bellanti, C. J., & Bierman, K. L. (1996). The quality of sibling relationships and the development of social competence and behavioral control in aggressive children. *Developmental Psychology, 32*, 79–89.

Stormshak, E. A., Comeau, C. A., & Shepard, S. A. (2004). The relative contribution of sibling deviance and peer deviance in the prediction of substance use across middle childhood. *Journal of Abnormal Child Psychology, 32*, 635–649.

Tucker, C. J., McHale, S. M., & Crouter, A. C. (2008). Links between older and younger adolescent siblings' adjustment: The moderating role of shared activities. *International Journal of Behavioral Development, 32,* 152–160.

Tucker, C. J., Updegraff, K. A., McHale, S. M., & Crouter, A. C. (1999). Older siblings as socializers of younger siblings' empathy. *Journal of Early Adolescence, 19,* 176–198.

Volling, B. L. (2003). Sibling relationships. In M. H. Bornstein, L. Davidson, L. M. Keyes, & K. A. Moore (Eds.), *Well-being: Positive development across the life course* (pp. 205–220). Mahwah, NJ: Erlbaum.

Vuchinich, S., Emery, R. E., & Cassidy, J. (1988). Family members and third parties in dyadic family conflict: Strategies, alliances, and outcomes. *Child Development, 59,* 1293–1302.

Widmer, E. D., & Weiss, C. C. (2000). Do older siblings make a difference? The effects of older sibling support and older sibling adjustment on the adjustment of socially disadvantaged adolescents. *Journal of Research on Adolescence, 10,* 1–27.

ELIZABETH A. STORMSHAK *is an associate professor of counseling psychology at the University of Oregon and codirector of the Child and Family Center, Eugene, Oregon. E-mail: bstorm@uoregon.edu.*

BERNADETTE M. BULLOCK *is a research scientist at the University of Oregon Child and Family Center, Eugene, Oregon. E-mail: bullock@uoregon.edu.*

CORINNA A. FALKENSTEIN *is a National Institute of Mental Health predoctoral trainee at the University of Oregon Child and Family Center, Eugene, Oregon. E-mail: cfalkens@uoregon.edu.*

NEW DIRECTIONS FOR CHILD AND ADOLESCENT DEVELOPMENT • DOI: 10.1002/cd

Jenkins, J., & Dunn, J. (2009). Siblings within families: Levels of analysis and patterns of influence. In L. Kramer & K. J. Conger (Eds.), *Siblings as agents of socialization*. New Directions for Child and Adolescent Development, 126, 79–93. San Francisco: Jossey-Bass.

6

Siblings Within Families: Levels of Analysis and Patterns of Influence

Jennifer Jenkins, Judy Dunn

Abstract

The study of siblings has become increasingly central to developmental science. Sibling relationships have unique effects on development, and sibling designs allow researchers to isolate causal mechanisms in development. This volume emphasizes causal mechanisms in the social domain. We review the preceding chapters in relation to six topics: a multilevel modeling approach to the ecology of sibling relationships, unique contributions of sibling relationships to development, sibling similarity and dissimilarity, developmental stages, culture and class, and intervention studies with siblings. We conclude with insights regarding directions for future research.© Wiley Periodicals, Inc.

NEW DIRECTIONS FOR CHILD AND ADOLESCENT DEVELOPMENT, NO. 126, WINTER 2009 © WILEY PERIODICALS, INC.
PUBLISHED ONLINE IN WILEY INTERSCIENCE (WWW.INTERSCIENCE.WILEY.COM) • DOI: 10.1002/cd.258

The study of siblings has become increasingly central to developmental science over recent years. The first reason for this relates to the role of relationship influences within families. The evidence based on methodologically strong designs that allow for causal inference, among them randomized control trials of parenting (DeGarmo, Forgatch, & Martinez, 1999), natural experiments (Costello, Compton, & Keeler, 2003), and longitudinal designs (Yagoubzadeh, Jenkins, & Pepler, in press), show unequivocally that individual development is shaped by our close relationships. Research on siblings has revealed that this particular relationship offers unique opportunities for development not provided by other close relationships. The second reason relates to the value of the sibling design for isolating causal mechanisms in development. Although the central goal of twin and sibling studies is to elucidate genetic influence, such designs have also been enormously helpful in demonstrating the role of the environment in children's behavior (Plomin, 1994). Consider, for instance, a design such as the monozygotic twin design, that includes a control for genetic influence. This provides a stronger case for relationship-based influences on behavior than designs that are not genetically sensitive (Caspi et al., 2004). Furthermore, the study of sibling similarity in monozygotic and dizygotic twins, and full siblings, reared together and reared apart, has allowed us to tease apart the influence of genes and distinguish between the role of the uterine environment and the postnatal home environment in IQ (Devlin, Daniels, & Roeder, 1997). Thus, sibling studies provide a critical means for identifying causal mechanisms, a goal that is central to developmental science (Rutter, Pickles, Murray, & Eaves, 2001).

As Kramer and Conger stress in Chapter One, the unique element of this volume is its emphasis on causal mechanisms in the social domain.

A Multilevel Approach to the Ecology of Sibling Relationships

The theoretical framework adopted by all of the chapter authors is an ecological one. The chapters differ on the breadth of the contextual effects that they describe. Chapters Three, Four, and Five are concerned with the family context, while others, including Chapter Two, are concerned with the broader ecological context in which the family is embedded. We too think that contextual effects are central to understanding sibling relationships. Furthermore, we suggest an even more specific operationalization of the ecological and systems models. In Chapter Five, Stormshak, Bullock, and Falkenstein used the term *multilevel* for their conceptual approach, and we elaborate this term both conceptually and analytically. The multilevel approach to families recognizes that children are nested within dyads, as well as within the family context as a whole. Families are, in turn, nested within macrostructures such as neighborhoods and ethnic communities. These data structures are best analyzed using a multilevel modeling approach specifically developed to examine clustering at different levels of the social environment. This is a technique that simultaneously allows the modeling of means and of variance (Goldstein, 1995; Rasbash, Steele, Browne, & Prosser, 2004).

The greatest advantage for sibling research of taking a multilevel approach is that all children in a family can be included in the sampling and analysis. Almost all current sibling research is focused on one sibling pair per family, as indicated by the previous chapters. This design has several limitations. First, if multiple dyads exist within the family, we may be incorrect in thinking that the processes that characterize one dyad characterize all dyads. In one study that included multiple dyads per family, we found that 48 percent of the variance in sibling relationships was within families (Jenkins, Dunn, O'Connor, Rasbash, & Behnke, 2005). Thus, although sibling dyads shared some similarities in relationship quality, they also differed markedly from one another. The second problem is that this design confounds sibling dyad and family effects. This is problematic for being able to conclude anything about the way in which context effects might operate. Consider the important finding, discussed in all chapters, that a close relationship between siblings when one child is deviant makes deviance in the other child more likely. Is the same effect seen across all dyads in the family (suggesting a family process), or is it restricted to one dyad (suggesting a process unique to the dyad)? Being able to discriminate between these two levels of context effect would give us a better understanding of the mechanisms underlying sibling socialization.

Predictor variables exist at different levels. Predictors such as the extent to which an individual child is monitored by his or her parents pertain to individual children. The quality of relationship between two siblings describes characteristics of the dyad, varying across different sibling dyads in the family. Predictors such as the presence of a child with a disability in the home, the ethnicity of the family, and the average level of monitoring done by the parents to the sibling group as a whole pertain to the whole family. In a multilevel model, these predictors are entered into the model to explain variance at the different levels of structure: between children, between dyads, and between families. This allows us to examine issues of shared and nonshared environments, as well as the relative roles of processes at different levels of the family environment.

One of the reasons for distinguishing between dyadic and family-level processes is to gain insight into the dynamics of families and the ways in which they affect sibling relationships. In one of our studies (Jenkins, Rasbash, Gass, & Dunn, 2009), we distinguished between the family average of maternal negativity (and positivity) directed to all children in the family and individual children's (both informants' and partners') deviation from the family average in predicting sibling relationship quality. For negativity, we found that the family average and children's individual deviations from the family mean both predicted relationship quality. For positivity, children's deviations from the family mean were more important in understanding sibling relationship quality than the family average. These findings raise the possibility that there are two sets of processes: one related to a whole family process, i.e., family climate, and a second related to comparisons between individuals. It may be that comparisons between siblings in the treatment that they are receiving from parents is central to both negativity and positivity as others have described (Brody, 1998) but that negativity in sibling relationships is also influenced by the general tone of family interactions. Margolin, Christensen and John (1996), as well as Katz and Gottman (1996), have described the ways in which negative affect from the marital dyad spills over into the affective quality of other relationships. Thus, it may be that negativity in dyadic relationships is more influenced by whole family processes than positivity.

A multilevel approach is also important for capturing interactions between macro- and microlevel processes. Bronfenbrenner (1977) cogently argued for the importance of taking into account macro- and microlevel processes when investigating influences on child development. Macrolevel processes have also been found to interact with microprocesses within families to explain children's outcomes and sibling relationships. For instance, we found that differential parenting of the members of a sibling dyad predicted sibling relationship quality only in single-parent families. Thus, in the macrocontext when parenting resources are limited, certain microprocesses specific to dyads (differential parenting) came into play (Jenkins, Dunn, et al., 2005). In a multilevel model, in which children are nested within dyads and families and families are nested within a macrocontext such as neighborhoods or ethnic communities, cross-level interactions can be readily investigated.

We offer one final thought about the importance of a multilevel framework for the investigation of sibling process. In each of the chapters, we see reference to component parts (sibling, parent-child, and marital dyads) and to the effects of individuals on one another (for example, deviant older siblings influencing the behavior of younger siblings). The most convincing means of separating individual, dyadic, and family effects is to use the social relations model (Kenny, 1994; Snijders & Kenny, 1999). Social relations model data are collected in a round-robin design in which all members of a family interact with one another. This data structure makes it possible to differentiate individual effects (the consistency of the way in which an individual behaves toward all of the people with whom he or she interacts, called an *actor effect,* and the behavior that the individual elicits from all of the people with whom he or she interacts, called a *partner effect*) from the influence of dyads, as well as the shared family influence. Such a design would allow us to establish what individual children take into their relationships with each of their siblings versus the dynamic that occurs because of the particular mixture of personalities in the dyad. Only one sibling pair has been included in social relation models to date (Manke & Pike, 2001; Ross,

Stein, Trabasso, Woody, & Ross, 2005), but we could learn a lot from the use of this design with a sibship that included three or six sibling dyads.

The Unique Opportunities for Development That the Sibling Relationship Offers

What is special about the relationships between siblings, and how do these relationships differ from children's relationships with their parents? Any attempt to address this question has to take on the striking individual differences in sibling relationships, evident in every study of siblings. Some relationships are warm and supportive, while others are hostile and difficult. The dimensions that Tucker and Updegraff highlight in Chapter Two—roles (complementary or reciprocal), emotional quality, caregiving, and support—are all important for children's outcomes, and sibling relationships differ markedly in these features.

There is one feature of sibling relationships, noted in Chapter One by Kramer and Conger, that is of key importance. This is the significance of sibling interactions for the growth of children's understanding of emotions and other minds—perhaps the hottest topic in cognitive development over the past two decades. The evidence for links between the extent to which children talk with siblings and friends about emotions, and engage in shared pretend, and children's later understanding of other minds and feelings—their grasp of theory of mind—is consistently reported (Dunn, 2004; Cutting & Dunn, 2006). The data are chiefly correlational, and thus drawing causal inferences from the associations is problematic. Nevertheless, the consistency of the links reported, and the evidence that such talk about others' feelings and inner states is much more frequent between siblings than between child and parent, is striking (Brown, Donelan-McCall, & Dunn, 1996). From these data, it appears that from the second year onward, a warm, conversational relationship with an older sibling can play a key part in the development of social understanding and that such talk is particularly frequent in the context of shared pretend play. This association is centrally important in children's development, and it highlights the significant role that certain kinds of sibling relationship can play in the early years of understanding others. Evidence for similar links of early friendships, understanding of mind, and the development of children's moral sensibility highlights the breadth and significance of later sequelae of child-child relationships (Hughes & Dunn, 1997; Dunn, Cutting, & Demetriou, 2000).

A critical point related to this is the nonshared environment in which a sibling pair grows up, even though the sibling relationship is a shared relationship. Jenkins, Turrell, Takai, Lollis, and Ross (2003) found that four-year-old children with an older sibling were exposed in the family environment to over twice the amount of cognitive talk (e.g., talk about thinking, remembering, knowing) than four-year-old children without an older sibling. This is because older siblings are responsible for much more talk about the feelings, thoughts, and beliefs of themselves and others than parents as this type of talk frequently occurs in the context of play. Without an older sibling, the child's exposure to this is much reduced. Differential exposure to mental state talk may be one of the reasons that children with older siblings show advanced theory of mind development (Lewis, Freeman, Kyriakidou, Maridaki-Kassataki, & Berridge, 1996). What then is the contribution of siblings to later stages of social understanding? This is another gap in what we know—an important gap to be filled.

Another unique aspect of the sibling relationship is its protective function for children in high-risk circumstances, a finding stressed by Kramer and Conger in Chapter One and Conger, Stocker, and McGuire in Chapter Four. When children are faced with family stresses, the presence of a close sibling relationship has been found to be associated with lower levels of disturbance in children (Gass, Jenkins, & Dunn, 2007; Jenkins, 1992). Interestingly, however, when the level of family stress is low, the quality of the sibling relationship is not associated with adjustment, suggesting that it plays a compensatory role in development. Given these results, the findings that Conger, Stocker, and McGuire report about the way in which siblings are often separated when they enter substitute care is disturbing. Although it is difficult to accommodate multiple children in foster care placements, we should also remember that not all children have close relationships with their siblings. When such relationships do exist, however, these findings suggest that keeping siblings together may reduce the considerable morbidity of foster care placement (Lawrence, Carlson, & Egeland, 2006) and lessen the need for postplacement intervention.

The effects of close sibling relationships can be both uniquely positive and uniquely negative. All of the chapter authors presented evidence that positive social relationships can be associated with sibling behavior problems (Slomkowski, Rende, Conger, Simons, & Conger, 2001; Stormshak, Comeau, & Shepard, 2004). Such associations have also been reported even with young children (Pike, Coldwell, & Dunn, 2005). At first sight, this appears at odds with the considerable evidence for prosocial outcomes following positive sibling interaction (East & Rook, 1992; Kim, McHale, Crouter, & Osgood, 2007; Stocker, 1994). But it does not conflict with everyday observations of siblings enjoying the fun of shared deviance as children and as adolescents (Bullock & Dishion, 2002; Criss & Shaw, 2005).

A further deleterious effect of the sibling relationship has been highlighted in the bullying literature. Wolke and his colleagues have shown that bullying occurs quite frequently within sibling relationships, and that children who are bullied by their siblings are significantly more likely to be bullied at school and suffer adjustment problems (Wolke & Samara, 2004). This is clearly a topic that deserves more attention, particularly because of the morbidity of victimization (Herba et al., 2008).

Sibling Similarity and Dissimilarity

One of the important contributions of this volume is its emphasis on the mechanisms involved in sibling similarity and dissimilarity. In Chapter Three, Whiteman, Becerra, and Killoren proposed deidentification as a central process in sibling dissimilarity. The basic premise is that in order to diminish competition between siblings for critical resources, a process of differentiation occurs. Previous studies on this issue have involved proxy variables to try to operationalize critical resources. Thus, several investigators have shown that siblings who are closer to one another in age, birth order, or the same gender show greater differentiation from one another as Whiteman, Becerra, and Killoren summarize. These authors' interesting contribution is to show that when asked, at least some siblings are able to give an account of the ways in which they try to differentiate themselves from their siblings.

It is important to remember, though, that there is a long history of experimental research in social psychology, starting with Nesbitt and Wilson (1977), that has shown that people are not accurate in describing their own motivations. The fact that children's conscious reports of differentiation explain some of the variance in sibling differences on behavior is a notable finding, but when interpreting this, we still face the issue of whether this is a post hoc explanation for sibling differences as opposed to a causal process. Although Whiteman, Becerra, and Killoren argue that the deidentification hypothesis is best assessed through self-report methodology, we would advocate continued use of indirect measurement (the term these authors use). We agree with the idea they propose that it is essential that the deidentification hypothesis be tested in families with more than one sibling pair. As discussed in the first section of this chapter, this is best done within the structure of a multilevel model in which we can examine the degree of similarity across different sibling dyads in the family, model similarity as a function of family and dyad processes, and explain variation between dyads and families.

We offer one final thought about deidentification. The theories that Whiteman, Becerra, and Killoren review all suggest that competition or rivalry is the motivating force behind deidentification. We think it likely that another motivating factor may be central. Younger siblings in the preschool period learn from watching their siblings in conflict interactions with their parents (Dunn, Brown, Slomkowski, Tesla, & Youngblade, 1991). Shanahan, McHale, Osgood, and Crouter (2007) have shown that the advent of adolescence is associated with a large rise in conflict with parents for first- but not second-born children. Perhaps through observational learning, second-born siblings figure out better ways of getting their goals met. The process of learning from siblings' mistakes is at the heart of several of Jane Austen's novels. For instance in *Sense and Sensibility*, Esther and Marianne watch one another's turmoil in matters of love. Each character develops through reflecting on the behavior that precipitates distress for her sibling.

We have carried out a series of studies related to sibling similarity and dissimilarity in data sets that include up to four children per family. In our opinion, one of the most important processes to consider is the multiplicative effect of environmental adversity. Tucker and Updegraff demonstrate in Chapter Two that many experiences at different levels of the environment can combine to influence development. In our work, we have found that siblings show greater differentiation from one another when environmental adversity is high (Jenkins & Bisceglia, in press; Jenkins, Simpson, Dunn, Rasbash, & O'Connor, 2005). Thus, more stressful environments seem to operate to spread siblings out on behavioral indexes. In part, the greater differentiation of siblings, as a function of environmental stress, can be explained by the way in which individual factors make children differentially vulnerable to shared environmental experiences. Factors such as children's achievement levels, physiological reactivity, and, perhaps most important, as Kramer and Conger point out in Chapter One, the unique ways in which they interpret environmental events have been shown to moderate the effects of adverse environments in single-child-per-family designs. They are also likely to explain differences between siblings in within family studies (Jenkins, 2008).

As all authors mention, the nonshared environment is critical to understanding sibling differences. Even environmental adversities that appear to be shared across all siblings, such as marital conflict, have a large nonshared component. So, for instance, the element of marital conflict found to be most damaging to a child is when the parents argue about him or her (Jenkins, Simpson, et al., 2005). Such argument is necessarily nonshared. Furthermore, it is important to remember that children contribute to the stressful environmental experiences that subsequently influence them (Yagoubzadeh et al., in press).

Developmental Stages

Tucker and Updegraff draw our attention in Chapter Two to other important gaps in what we know about the relative importance of sibling and parent-child relationships over time, for instance, in the relative support provided by siblings and parents as children grow up. The evidence they discuss indicates important differences in how developmental changes differ in these aspects of the two relationships: parental support, they suggest, decreases over adolescence, while sibling support is stable over this period.

The potential for both older and younger siblings to exert influence on each other is important to acknowledge, and here the developmental changes in younger siblings' understanding of others are important. As children grow and mature in the sensitivity of their understanding of others, their potential influence on their older sibling increases—for both good and for evil! In a longitudinal study in Cambridge, England, we found that preschoolers' negative behavior toward their older siblings was associated with poor outcomes for their older siblings over the ensuing years (Dunn, Slomkowski, & Beardsall, 1994).

NEW DIRECTIONS FOR CHILD AND ADOLESCENT DEVELOPMENT • DOI: 10.1002/cd

Further examples of developmental change in the siblings associated with changes in the quality of the dyadic relationship were highlighted in the Cambridge longitudinal study. First, both sibling and mothers described negative changes in the sibling relationship, which they attributed to the new friendships formed by the children outside the family, through school. These friendships were seen as contributing to either increased jealousy or decreased closeness between the siblings. And the majority of children considered changes in their sibling relationships to be related to the second-borns' growing powers of argument, his or her increasing assertiveness, and the development of different interests. In a majority of families, the children grew closer, with an increase in affectionate behavior, in the face of adverse life events (Dunn et al., 1994). We need to study the more minor stressful events and changes in the sibling relationship too. Frequent daily hassles have been found to be linked to siblings' accounts of a lack of intimacy years later.

Culture and Class

Differences in culture were mentioned throughout the volume, usually to emphasize the narrow sampling that is the basis of many sibling studies. The authors stress the importance of widening the framework of sibling research to include non-Western families. This is likely to be particularly important in relation to the connections between parental and sibling relations. Tucker and Updegraff show in Chapter Two that the amount of time that siblings spend together differs across cultures, with evidence that older siblings take on a parental role in some cultures. Thus, parental and sibling supports appear to differ across cultures. They further speculate that sibling processes may have a different relationship to individual children's adjustment in different cultures. Given that parent-to-child warmth and harshness have been found to be differentially related to children's outcomes as a function of ethnic group (Deater-Deckard, Dodge, Bates, & Pettit, 1996; Ho, Bluestein, & Jenkins, 2008), we agree that this represents a very important area of investigation in sibling research.

And even studies within the same culture can demonstrate that developmental changes can be linked to social class. In our longitudinal research in Cambridge, the increasing impact of social class was evident as the children reached adolescence. In the preschool period, there were relatively few associations between the quality of sibling relations and social class. But by early adolescence, gender and lower social class were associated with poorer relations between older boys and younger sisters, as the boys spent more time away from their families and with their peer group (Dunn, 1996).

Economic issues affecting families did not feature prominently in the chapters. We think, however, that this is a topic of central importance to the study of siblings. Evidence suggests that income differentials within a society (the amount earned by the bottom 20 percent of the population compared to the top 20 percent of the society) is a powerful predictor of many aspects of well-being (Wilkinson & Pickett, 2009). In countries with very high income differentials (such as the United States and the United Kingdom), child outcomes are more compromised than those countries with lower differentials (such as Japan and Sweden).

The process of differential access to resources seen at the societal level has a parallel within families. One of the most replicated findings in sibling research is that higher differential warmth or hostility directed to the two children in a sibling dyad predicts the quality of the children's relationship with one another (see Tucker and Updegraff in Chapter Two). This effect is driven more by children's perceptions of the fairness of parental behavior (Kowal & Kramer, 1997) than by the parental behavior itself. Even more intriguing is the finding that when the family itself is characterized by higher levels of differential behavior across siblings, children's behavior is more compromised. Boyle et al. (2004) distinguished between differential parenting received by individuals (the individual's departure from the family average in families with multiple children) and the family average for differential parenting (the average differential across all children in the family). They found that when the family average of differential parenting was higher, the average level of behavioral problems in the family was also higher, even after accounting for the differential experienced by individuals. Furthermore, Jenkins, Rasbash, and O'Connor (2003) found that as economic disadvantage increased, differential parenting also increased. Together these findings suggest that the fair allocation of resources within societies is linked to the fair allocation of resources within families and that both are likely to matter to the development of good family relationships.

Intervention Studies with Siblings

Intervention studies that involve random assignment to condition allow one to draw conclusions about causal process that are not justified on the basis of correlational designs. Thus, when Kennedy and Kramer (2008) show that an intervention geared toward improving children's emotion regulation skills, in which children were randomly assigned to the intervention or a waiting list control, results in improved sibling relationships in children between four and eight years of age, we can conclude that emotion regulation processes are central to ongoing relationship quality between siblings. The integration of correlational and experimental data in the volume is a real strength.

The intervention described in Chapter Five by Stormshak, Bullock, and Falkenstein offers important information about the generalizability of parenting interventions to multiple children in the family. Although the intervention is geared to one parent-child relationship, other children also benefit. Brotman et al. (2005) report a similar phenomenon such that intervention involving parents and an older delinquent child can prevent problems in younger siblings years later. Research on the parenting of multiple children per family shows (depending on the measurement) that about one-third to one-half of the variance in parenting is shared (O'Connor, Dunn, Jenkins, & Rasbash, 2006), leaving a large proportion that is specific to individual children. Different children in the family, with their different temperaments, elicit unique parental responses (O'Connor, 2002). It is interesting, then, that the intervention that Stormshak, Bullock, and Falkenstein describe is generalized upward, such that parents implement the altered parental practices across all their children. This result offers some justification for psychoeducational parenting programs. These programs generally conceptualize parenting (incorrectly!) as a construct that is invariant across all children. Some of the efficacy of these programs, however, may derive from the parents' forming principles of behavior that become invariant across children (for example, all children need to be monitored or responded to with warmth and praise). Because the results by Stormshak, Bullock, and Falkenstein have not been fully reported, it will be very beneficial to consider a multilevel approach to the data analysis. This would enable us to examine the extent to which parenting starts out as child specific and changes to more of a shared phenomenon as a result of intervention.

We support Stormshak, Bullock, and Falkenstein's discussion of individualized goals for intervention research. In this spirit, though, we add that therapeutic goals may not always be compatible with one another. Although several research groups have found that close relationships with delinquent adolescent siblings lead to delinquency in the younger sibling, we do have to consider the downside of decreasing contact between siblings. The comorbidity of anxiety and depression with externalizing behavior is considerable in adolescence. Intervention research tends to focus on one goal (say, decreasing delinquency), but in the context of the child's ongoing development, multiple goals may be important. Given that externalizing children are more likely to come from family environments that are nonoptimal, with, for example, high levels of parent-child hostility, marital conflict, or parental indifference, discouraging the child's only warm and intimate relationship may have a negative consequence for other aspects of functioning. Thus, it is important to keep in mind the multiplicity of goals that may operate for vulnerable children living in adverse environments.

Future Directions for Research

The authors in this volume have shown that sibling designs are helpful in elucidating causal processes in development. As we move forward, certain kinds of studies hold particular promise. First, the inclusion of more than one sibling dyad per family will help to improve our understanding of family processes, as well as the role of individual, dyadic, and family effects in development. Second, as the work in this volume illustrates, siblings offer opportunities for development, both positive and negative, not offered by other relationships. An understanding of the developmental context of these unique influences is needed. Are siblings central to children's understanding of other minds only in the preschool period, or is this relationship equally important to such understanding in adolescence? Third, as all authors showed, environmental influences on child development are complex, with both independent and interactive effects across multiple levels of children's contexts. Designs that allow this complexity will be important. Fourth, although intervention studies are challenging to do well, their payoff in terms of understanding causal process is high. Furthermore, following the example of Conger, Stocker, and McGuire in Chapter Four, we can use our knowledge of sibling relationships to consider the ways in which children's lives in high-risk environments might be improved.

References

Boyle, M. H., Jenkins, J. M., Hadjiyannakis, K., Cairney, J., Duku, E., & Racine, Y. A. (2004). Family differential parenting: Estimating within and between family effects on children. *Child Development*, 75, 1457–1476.

Brody, G. H. (1998). Sibling relationship quality: Its causes and consequences. *Annual Review of Psychology*, 49, 1–24.

Bronfenbrenner, U. (1977). Toward an experimental ecology of human development. *American Psychologist*, 32, 513–531.

Brotman, L. M., Dawson-McClure, S., Gouley, K. K., McGuire, K., Burraston, B., & Bank, L. (2005). Older siblings benefit from a family-based preventive intervention for preschoolers at risk for conduct problems. *Journal of Family Psychology*, 19, 581–591.

Brown, J., Donelan-McCall, N., & Dunn, J. (1996). Why talk about mental states? The significance of children's conversations with friends, siblings, and mothers. *Child Development*, 67, 836–849.

Bullock, B. M., & Dishion, T. (2002). Sibling collusion and problem behavior in early adolescence: Toward a process model for family mutuality. *Journal of Abnormal Child Psychology*, 30, 143–153.

Caspi, A., Moffitt, T. E., Morgan, J., Rutter, M., Taylor, A., Arseneault, L., et al. (2004). Maternal expressed emotion predicts children's antisocial behavior problems: Using MZ twin differences to identify environmental effects on behavioral development. *Developmental Psychology*, 40, 149–161.

Costello, J. E., Compton, S. N., & Keeler, G. (2003). Relationship between poverty and psychopathology: A natural experiment. *Journal of American Medical Association*, 290, 2023–2029.

Criss, M. M., & Shaw, D. S. (2005) Sibling relationships as contexts for delinquency training in low income families. *Journal of Family Psychology*, 19, 592–600.

Cutting, A. L., & Dunn, J. (2006). Conversations with siblings and with friends: Links between relationship quality and social understanding. *British Journal of Developmental Psychology*, 24, 73–87.

Deater-Deckard, K., Dodge, K. A., Bates, J. E., & Pettit, G. S. (1996). Physical discipline among African American and European American mothers: Links to children's externalizing behaviors. *Developmental Psychology*, 32, 1065–1072.

DeGarmo, D. S., Forgatch, M. S., & Martinez, C. R., Jr. (1999). Parenting of divorced mothers as a link between social status and boys' academic outcomes: Unpacking the effects of socioeconomic status. *Child Development*, 70, 1231–1245.

Devlin, B., Daniels, M., & Roeder, K. (1997). The heritability of IQ. *Nature*, 388, 468–471.

Dunn, J. (1996). Brothers and sisters in middle childhood and early adolescence: Continuity and change in individual differences. In G. H. Brody (Ed.), *Sibling relationships: Their causes and consequences* (pp. 31–46). Norwood, NJ: Ablex.

Dunn, J. (2004). The development of individual differences in understanding emotion and mind: Antecedents and sequelae. In A. Manstead (Ed.), *Amsterdam Conference on Feelings and Emotions* (pp. 303–320). Cambridge: Cambridge University Press.

Dunn, J., Brown, J., Slomkowski, C., Tesla, C., & Youngblade, L. (1991). Young children's understanding of other people's feelings and beliefs: Individual differences and their antecedents. *Child Development, 62*, 1352–1366.

Dunn, J., Cutting, A., & Demetriou, H. (2000). Moral sensibility, understanding others, and friendship interactions in the preschool period. *British Journal of Developmental Psychology, 18*, 159–177.

Dunn, J., Slomkowski, C., & Beardsall, L. (1994). Sibling relationships from the preschool period through middle childhood and early adolescence. *Developmental Psychology, 30*, 315–324.

East, P. L., & Rook, K. S. (1992). Compensatory patterns of support among children's peer relationships: A test using friends, nonschool friends and siblings. *Developmental Psychology, 21*, 1016–1024.

Gass, K., Jenkins, J. M., & Dunn, J. (2007). The sibling relationship as protective for children experiencing life events: A longitudinal study. *Journal of Child Psychology and Psychiatry, 48*, 167–175.

Goldstein, H. M. (1995). *Multilevel statistical models*. London: Edward Arnold.

Herba, C. M., Ferdinand, R. F., Stijnen, T., Veenstra, R., Oldehinkel, A., Ormel, J., et al. (2008). Victimisation and suicide ideation in the trails study: Specific vulnerabilities of victims. *Journal of Child Psychology and Psychiatry, 49*, 867–876.

Ho, C., Bluestein, D. N., & Jenkins, J. (2008). Cultural differences in the relationship between parenting and children's behavior. *Developmental Psychology, 44*, 507–522.

Hughes, C., & Dunn, J. (1997). "Pretend you didn't know": Preschoolers' talk about mental states in pretend play. *Cognitive Development, 12*, 477–497.

Jenkins, J. (1992). Sibling relationships in disharmonious homes: Potential difficulties and protective effects. In F. Boer & J. Dunn (Eds.), *Children's sibling relationships: Developmental and clinical issues* (pp. 125–138). Hillsdale, NJ: Erlbaum.

Jenkins, J. M. (2008). Psychosocial adversity and resilience. In M. Rutter, D. Bishop, D. Pin, S. Scott, J. Stevenson, E. A. Taylor, et al. (Eds.), *Rutters' handbook of child and adolescent psychiatry* (5th ed.). Oxford: Blackwell.

Jenkins, J. M., & Bisceglia, R. (in press). Understanding within-family variability in children's responses to environmental stress. In D. P. Keating (Ed.), *Nature and nurture in early child development*. Cambridge: Cambridge University Press.

Jenkins, J., Dunn, J., O'Connor, T. G., Rasbash, J., & Behnke, P. (2005). Change in maternal perception of sibling negativity: Within and between family influences. *Journal of Family Psychology, 19*, 533–541.

Jenkins, J., Rasbash, J., Gass, K., & Dunn, J. (2009). *The multilevel dynamics of sibling relationships: Influences over time*. Manuscript submitted for publication.

Jenkins, J. M., Rasbash, J., & O'Connor, T. G. (2003). The role of the shared family context in differential parenting. *Developmental Psychology, 39*, 99–113.

Jenkins, J. M., Simpson, A., Dunn, J., Rasbash, J., & O'Connor, T. G. (2005). The mutual influence of marital conflict and children's behavior problems: Shared and non-shared family risks. *Child Development, 76*, 24–39.

Jenkins, J. M., Turrell, S., Takai, Y., Lollis, S., & Ross, H. (2003). Longitudinal investigation of the dynamics of mental state talk in families. *Child Development, 74*, 905–920.

Katz, L. F., & Gottman, J. M. (1996). Spillover effects of marital conflict: In search of parenting and coparenting mechanisms. In J. P. McHale & P. A. Cowan (Eds.), *Understanding how family-level dynamics affect children's development: Studies of two-parent families. New Directions for Child Development*, (Vol. 74, pp. 57–76). San Francisco, CA: Jossey-Bass.

Kennedy, D. E., & Kramer, L. (2008). Improving emotion regulation and sibling relationship quality: The More Fun with Sisters and Brothers Program. *Family Relations, 57*, 568–579.

Kenny, D. A. (1994). Using the social relations model to understand relationships. In R. Erber & R. Gilmour (Eds.), *Theoretical frameworks for personal relationships* (pp. 111–127). Hillsdale, NJ: Erlbaum.

Kim, J.-Y., McHale, S. M., Crouter, A. C., & Osgood, D. W. (2007). Longitudinal linkages between sibling relationships and adjustment from middle childhood through adolescence. *Developmental Psychology, 43*, 960–973.

Kowal, A., & Kramer, L. (1997). Children's understanding of parental differential treatment. *Child Development, 68*, 113–126.

Lawrence, C. R., Carlson, E. A., & Egeland, B. (2006). The impact of foster care on development. *Development and Psychopathology, 18*, 57–76.

Lewis, C., Freeman, N. H., Kyriakidou, C., Maridaki-Kassataki, K., & Berridge, M. D. (1996). Social influences on false belief access: Specific sibling influences or general apprenticeship. *Child Development, 67*, 2930–2947.

Manke, B., & Pike, A. (2001). Combining the social relations model and behavioral genetics to explore the etiology of familial interactions. *Marriage and Family Review, 33*, 179–204.

Margolin, G., Christensen, A., & John, R. S. (1996). The continuance and spillover of everyday tensions in distressed and nondistressed families. *Journal of Family Psychology, 10*, 304–321.

Nesbitt, R. E., & Wilson, T. D. (1977).Telling more than we can know: Verbal reports on mental processes. *Psychological Review, 84*, 231–259.

O'Connor, T. G. (2002). Annotation: The "effects" of parenting reconsidered: Findings, challenges, and applications. *Journal of Child Psychology and Psychiatry and Allied Disciplines, 43*, 555–572.

O'Connor, T. G., Dunn, J., Jenkins, J. M., & Rasbash, J. (2006). Predictors of between-family and within-family variation in parent-child relationships. *Journal of Child Psychology and Psychiatry, 47*, 498–510.

Pike, A., Coldwell, J., & Dunn, J. F. (2005). Sibling relationships in early/middle childhood: Links with individual adjustment. *Journal of Family Psychology, 19*, 523–529.

Plomin, R. (1994). *Genetics and experience.* Thousand Oaks, CA: Sage.

Rasbash, J., Steele, F., Browne, W. J., & Prosser, B. (2004). *A user's guide to MLwiN, Version 2.0.* London: Institute of Education.

Ross, H., Stein, N., Trabasso, T., Woody, E., & Ross, M. (2005). The quality of family relationships within and across generations: A social relations analysis. *International Journal of Behavioral Development, 29*, 110–119.

Rutter, M., Pickles, A., Murray, R., & Eaves, L. (2001). Testing hypotheses on specific environmental causal effects on behavior. *Psychological Bulletin, 127*, 291–324.

Shanahan, L., McHale, S., Osgood, W., & Crouter, A. C. (2007). Conflict frequency with mothers and fathers from middle childhood to late adolescence: Within- and between-families comparisons. *Developmental Psychology, 43*, 539–550.

Slomkowski, C., Rende, R., Conger, K. J., Simons, R. L., & Conger, R. D. (2001). Sisters, brothers, and delinquency: Evaluating social influence during early and middle adolescence. *Child Development, 72*, 271–283.

Snijders, T., & Kenny, D. A. (1999). The social relations model for family data: A multilevel approach. *Personal Relationships, 6*, 471–486.

Stocker, C. M. (1994). Children's perceptions of relationships with siblings, friends, and mothers: Compensatory processes and links with adjustment. *Journal of Child Psychology and Psychiatry, 35*, 1447–1459.

Stormshak, E. A., Comeau, C. A., & Shepard, S. A. (2004). The relative contribution of sibling deviance and peer deviance in the prediction of substance use across middle childhood. *Journal of Abnormal Child Psychology, 32*, 635–649.

Wilkinson, R., & Pickett, K. (2009). *The spirit level*. London: Penguin Books.

Wolke, D., & Samara, M. M. (2004). Bullied by siblings: Association with peer victimisation and behaviour problems in Israeli lower secondary school children. *Journal of Child Psychology and Psychiatry, 45*, 1015–1029.

Yagoubzadeh, Z., Jenkins, J. M., & Pepler, D. (in press). Transactional models in the relationship between child behavior and maternal negativity: A six-year longitudinal study. *International Journal of Behavioral Development*.

JENNIFER JENKINS is professor of human development and applied psychology at the University of Toronto, Toronto, Canada. E-mail: jenny.jenkins@utoronto.ca.

JUDY DUNN is professor of developmental psychology at the Social, Genetic and Developmental Psychiatry Research Centre, Institute of Psychiatry, King's College, University of London, London. E-mail: judith.dunn@kcl.ac.uk.

NEW DIRECTIONS FOR CHILD AND ADOLESCENT DEVELOPMENT • DOI: 10.1002/cd

INDEX

integration of regulatory subsystems, the emergence of autonomous regulation, and the progressive construction of the kinds of regulatory resources and routines that allow flexible constructive coping under successively higher levels of stress and adversity. All chapters emphasize the importance of integrative multilevel perspectives in bringing together work on the neurobiology of stress, temperament, attachment, regulation, personal resources, relationships, stress exposure, and social contexts in studying processes of coping, adversity, and resilience.
ISBN 978-04705-31372

CAD 123 *Social Interaction and the Development of Executive Function*
Charlie Lewis, Jeremy I. M. Carpendale
Executive function consists of higher cognitive skills that are involved in the control of thought, action, and emotion. It has been linked to neural systems involving the prefrontal cortex, but a full definition of the term has remained elusive partly because it includes such a complex set of cognitive processes. Relatively little is known about the processes that promote development of executive function, and how it is linked to children's social behavior. The key factor examined by the chapters in this issue is the role of social interaction, and the chapters take an increasingly broad perspective. Two end pieces introduce the topic as a whole (Chapter 1) and present an integrative commentary on the articles (Chapter 6) in an attempt to stress the social origins of executive function, in contrast to many contemporary cognitive approaches. The empirical contributions in between examine the roles of parental scaffolding of young preschoolers (Chapter 2), the links between maternal education and conversational support (Chapter 3), how such family background factors and social skills extend into adolescence (Chapter 4), and wider cultural influences (Chapter 5) on development of executive skills. This volume is aimed at a broad range of developmental researchers and practitioners interested in the influences of family background and inter-actions as well as educational and cultural processes on development of the child's self-control and social understanding. Such relationships have wide implications for many aspects of the lives of children and adolescents.
ISBN 978-04704-89017

CAD 122 *Core Competencies to Prevent Problem Behaviors and Promote Positive Youth Development*
Nancy G. Guerra, Catherine P. Bradshaw, Editors
Adolescence generally is considered a time of experimentation and increased involvement in risk or problem behaviors, including early school leaving, violence, substance use, and high-risk sexual behavior. In this volume, the authors show how individual competencies linked to well-being can reduce youth involvement in these risk behaviors. Five core competencies are emphasized: a positive sense of self, self-control, decision-making skills, a moral system of belief, and prosocial connectedness. A central premise of this volume is that high levels of the core competencies provide a marker for positive youth development, whereas low levels increase the likelihood of adolescent risk behavior. The authors summarize the empirical literature linking these competencies to each risk behavior, providing examples from developmental and prevention research. They highlight programs and poli-cies in the United States and internationally that have changed one or more dimensions of the core competencies through efforts designed to build indi-vidual skills, strengthen relationships, and enhance opportunities and sup-ports across multiple developmental contexts.
ISBN 978-04704-42166

CAD 121 **Beyond the Family: Contexts of Immigrant Children's Development**
Hirokazu Yoshikawa, Niobe Way, Editors
Immigration in the United States has become a central focus of policy and
public concern in the first decade of the 21st century. This volume aims to
broaden developmental research on children and youth in immigrant families. Much of the research on immigrant children and youth concentrates on
family characteristics such as parenting, demographic, or human capital features. In this volume, we consider the developmental consequences for immigrant youth of broader contexts such as social networks, peer discrimination
in school and out-of-school settings, legal contexts, and access to institutional
resources. Chapters answer questions such as: How do experiences of discrimination affect the lives of immigrant youth? How do social networks of
immigrant families influence children's learning? How do immigrant parents'
citizenship status influence family life and their children's development? In
examining factors as disparate as discrimination based on physical appear-
ance, informal adult helpers, and access to drivers' licenses, these chapters
serve to enrich our notions of how culture and context shape human development, as well as inform practice and public policy affecting immigrant families.
ISBN 978-04704-17300

CAD 120 **The Intersections of Personal and Social Identities**
Margarita Azmitia, Moin Syed, Kimberley Radmacher, Editors
This volume brings together an interdisciplinary set of social scientists who
are pioneering ways to research and theorize the connections between
personal and social identity development in children, adolescents, and
emerging adults. The authors of the seven chapters address the volume's three
goals: (1) illustrating how theory and research in identity develop-ment are
enriched by an interdisciplinary approach, (2) providing a rich developmental
picture of personal and social identity development, and (3) examining the
connections among multiple identities. Several chapters provide practical
suggestions for individuals, agencies, and schools and universities that work
with children, adolescents, and emerging adults in diverse communities across
the United States.
ISBN 978-04703-72838

CAD 119 **Social Class and Transitions to Adulthood**
Jeylan T. Mortimer, Editor
This volume of *New Directions for Child and Adolescent Development* is inspired
by a stirring address that Frank Furstenberg delivered at the 2006 Meeting of
the Society for Research on Adolescence, "Diverging Development: The Not
So Invisible Hand of Social Class in the United States." He called on social
scientists interested in the study of development to expand their purview
beyond investigations of the developmental impacts of poverty and consider
the full gamut of social class variation in our increasingly unequal society.
The gradations of class alter the social supports, resources, and opportunities,
as well as the constraints, facing parents as they attempt to guide their
children toward the acquisition of adult roles. This volume examines the
impacts of social class origin on the highly formative period of transition to
adulthood. Drawing on findings from the Youth Development Study and other
sources, the authors examine social class differences in adult child–parent
relationships, intimacy and family formation, attainment of higher education,
the school-to-work transition, the emergence of work-family conflict, and
harassment in the workplace. The authors indicate new directions for research
that will contribute to understanding the problems facing young people today.

These chapters will persuade those making social policy to develop social interventions that will level the playing field and increase the opportunities for disadvantaged youth to become healthy and productive adults.
ISBN 978-04702-93621

CAD 118 *Social Network Analysis and Children's Peer Relationships*
Philip C. Rodkin, Laura D. Hanish, Editors
Social network analysis makes it possible to determine how large and dense children's peer networks are, how central children are within their networks, the various structural configurations that characterize social groups, and which peers make up individual children's networks. By centering the child within his or her social system, it is possible to understand the socialization processes that draw children toward or away from particular peers, as well as those who contribute to peer influence. This volume of *New Directions for Child and Adolescent Development* demonstrates how social network analysis provides insights into the ways in which peer groups contribute to children's and adolescents' development—from gender and intergroup relations, to aggression and bullying, to academic achievement. Together the chapters in this volume depict the complex, nested, and dynamic structure of peer groups and explain how social structure defines developmental processes.
ISBN 978-04702-59665

CAD 117 *Attachment in Adolescence: Reflections and New Angles*
Miri Scharf, Ofra Mayseless, Editors
In recent years, the number of empirical studies examining attachment in adolescence has grown considerably, with most focusing on individual differences in attachment security. This volume goes a step further in extending our knowledge and understanding. The physical, cognitive, emotional, and social changes that characterize adolescence invite a closer conceptual look at attachment processes and organization during this period. The chapter authors, leading researchers in attachment in adolescence, address key topics in attachment processes in adolescence. These include issues such as the normative distancing from parents and the growing importance of peers, the formation of varied attachment hierarchies, the changing nature of attachment dynamics from issues of survival to issues of affect regulation, siblings' similarity in attachment representations, individual differences in social information processes in adolescence, and stability and change in attachment representations in a risk sample. Together the chapters provide a compelling discussion of intriguing issues and broaden our understanding of attachment in adolescence and the basic tenets of attachment theory at large.
ISBN 978-04702-25608

CAD 116 *Linking Parents and Family to Adolescent Peer Relations: Ethnic and Cultural Considerations*
B. Bradford Brown, Nina S. Mounts, Editors
Ethnic and cultural background shapes young people's development and behavior in a variety of ways, including their interactions with family and peers. The intersection of family and peer worlds during childhood has been studied extensively, but only recently has this work been extended to adolescence. This volume of *New Directions for Child and Adolescent Development* highlights new research linking family to adolescent peer relations from a multiethnic perspective. Using qualitative and quantitative research methods, the contributors consider similarities and differences within and between ethnic groups in regard to several issues: parents' goals and strategies for guiding young people to adaptive peer relationships, how peer relationships shape

and are shaped by kin relationships, and the specific strategies that adolescents and parents use to manage information about peers or negotiate rules about peer interactions and relationships. Findings emphasize the central role played by sociocultural context in shaping the complex, bidirectional processes that link family members to adolescents' peer social experiences.
ISBN 978-04701-78010

CAD 115 **Conventionality in Cognitive Development: How Children Acquire Shared Representations in Language, Thought, and Action**
Chuck W. Kalish, Mark A. Sabbagh, Editors
An important part of cognitive development is coming to think in culturally normative ways. Children learn the right names for objects, proper functions for tools, appropriate ways to categorize, and the rules for games. In each of these cases, what makes a given practice normative is not naturally given. There is not necessarily any objectively better or worse way to do any of these things. Instead, what makes them correct is that people agree on how they should be done, and each of these practices therefore has an important conventional basis. The chapters in this volume highlight the fact that successful participation in practices of language, cognition, and play depends on children's ability to acquire representations that other members of their social worlds share. Each of these domains poses problems of identifying normative standards and achieving coordination across agents. This volume brings together scholars from diverse areas in cognitive development to consider the psychological mechanisms supporting the use and acquisition of conventional knowledge.
ISBN 978-07879-96970

CAD 114 **Respect and Disrespect: Cultural and Developmental Origins**
David W. Schwalb, Barbara J. Schwalb, Editors
Respect enables children and teenagers to value other people, institutions, traditions, and themselves. Disrespect is the agent that dissolves positive relationships and fosters hostile and cynical relationships. Unfortunately, parents, educators, children, and adolescents in many societies note with alarm a growing problem of disrespect and a decline in respect for self and others. Is this disturbing trend a worldwide problem? To answer this question, we must begin to study the developmental and cultural origins of respect and disrespect. Five research teams report that respect and disrespect are influenced by experiences in the family, school, community, and, most importantly, the broader cultural setting. The chapters introduce a new topic area for mainstream developmental sciences that is relevant to the interests of scholars, educators, practitioners, and policymakers.
ISBN 978-07879-95584

CAD 113 **The Modernization of Youth Transitions in Europe**
Manuela du Bois-Reymond, Lynne Chisholm, Editors
This compelling volume focuses on what it is like to be young in the rapidly changing, enormously diverse world region that is early 21st century Europe. Designed for a North American readership interested in youth and young adulthood, *The Modernization of Youth Transitions in Europe* provides a rich fund of theoretical insight and empirical evidence about the implications of contemporary modernization processes for young people living, learning, and working across Europe. Chapters have been specially written for this volume by well-known youth sociologists; they cover a wide range of themes against a shared background of the reshaping of the life course and its constituent phases toward greater openness and contigency. New modes of learning accompany complex routes into employment and career under rapidly

changing labor market conditions and occupational profiles, while at the same time new family and lifestyle forms are developing alongside greater intergenerational responsibilities in the face of the retreat of the modern welfare state. The complex patterns of change for today's young Europeans are set into a broader framework that analyzes the emergence and character of European youth research and youth policy in recent years.
ISBN 978-07879-88890

CAD 112 **Rethinking Positive Adolescent Female Sexual Development**
Lisa M. Diamond, Editor
This volume provides thoughtful and diverse perspectives on female adolescent sexuality. These perspectives integrate biological, cultural, and interpersonal influences on adolescent girls' sexuality, and highlight the importance of using multiple methods to investigate sexual ideation and experience. Traditional portrayals cast adolescent females as sexual gatekeepers whose primary task is to fend off boys' sexual overtures and set aside their own sexual desires in order to reduce their risks for pregnancy and sexually transmitted diseases. Yet an increasing number of thoughtful and constructive critiques have challenged this perspective, arguing for more sensitive, in-depth, multimethod investigations into the positive meanings of sexuality for adolescent girls that will allow us to conceptualize (and, ideally, advocate for) healthy sexual-developmental trajectories. Collectively, authors of this volume take up this movement and chart exciting new directions for the next generation of developmental research on adolescent female sexuality.
ISBN 978-07879-87350

CAD 111 **Family Mealtime as a Context for Development and Socialization**
Reed W. Larson, Angela R. Wiley, Kathryn R. Branscomb, Editors
This issue examines the impact of family mealtime on the psychological development of young people. In the popular media, family mealtime is often presented as a vital institution for the socialization and development of young people, but also as one that is "going the way of the dinosaur." Although elements such as fast food and TV have become a part of many family mealtimes, evidence is beginning to suggest that mealtimes can also provide rich opportunities for children's and adolescents' development. While what happens at mealtimes varies greatly among families, an outline of the forms and functions of mealtimes is beginning to emerge from this research. In this issue, leading mealtime researchers from the fields of history, cultural anthropology, psycholinguistics, psychology, and nutrition critically review findings from each of their disciplines, giving primary focus on family mealtimes in the United States. The authors in this issue examine the history of family mealtimes, describe contemporary mealtime practices, elucidate the differing transactional processes that occur, and evaluate evidence on the outcomes associated with family mealtimes from children and adolescents.
ISBN 978-07879-85776

CAD 110 **Leaks in the Pipeline to Math, Science, and Technology Careers**
Janis E. Jacobs, Sandra D. Simpkins, Editors
Around the world, the need for highly trained scientists and technicians remains high, especially for positions that require employees to have a college degree and skills in math, science, and technology. The pipeline into these jobs begins in high school, but many "leaks" occur before young people reach the highly educated workforce needed to sustain leadership in science and technology. Students drop out of the educational pipeline in science and technology at alarming rates at each educational transition beginning in

high school, but women and ethnic minority youth drop out at a faster rate. Women and minorities are consistently underrepresented in science and engineering courses and majors. They account for a small portion of the work force in high-paying and more innovative jobs that require advanced degrees. This schism between the skills necessary in our ever-changing economy and the skill set that most young adults acquire is troubling. It leads us to ask the question that forms the basis for this issue: Why are adolescents and young adults, particularly women and minorities, opting out of the math, science, and technology pipeline? The volume addresses gender and ethnic differences in the math, science, and technology pipeline from multiple approaches, including theoretical perspectives, a review of the work in this field, presentation of findings from four longitudinal studies, and a discussion of research implications given the current educational and economic climate.
ISBN 978-07879-83932

CAD 109 *New Horizons in Developmental Theory and Research*
Lene Arnett Jensen, Reed W. Larson, Editors
This inaugural issue by the new editors-in-chief brings together a group of cutting-edge developmental scholars who each report on promising new lines of theory and research within their specialty areas. Their essays cover a selection of important topics including emotion-regulation, family socialization, friendship, self, civic engagement, media, and culture. In the succinct, engaging essays, all authors provide thought-provoking views of the horizons in the field.
ISBN 978-07879-83413

CAD 108 *Changing Boundaries of Parental Authority During Adolescence*
Judith Smetena, Editor
This volume describes research focusing on changes in different dimensions of parenting and conceptions of parental authority during adolescence. The seven chapters illuminate the dimensions of parenting that change (or remain stable) over the course of adolescence. The chapters also ighlight the importance of considering variations in parenting accoding to the different domains of adolescents' lives, their relationships to the development of responsibility automony, and how these are influenced by socioeconomic status, culture, and ethnicity. Thus, the chapters in this volume provide new directions for conceptualizing variations in parenting over the second decade of life and their implicaions for adolescent adjustment and well-being. The authors point to the need for developmentally sensitive models of parenting that consider changes within domains over time, their influence on adolescent development and functioning, and potential asynchronies between parents and adolescents.
ISBN 978-07879-81921

CAD 107 *The Experience of Close Friendship in Adolescence*
Niobe Way, Jill V. Hamm, Editors
In this issue, we present findings from four studies that employed qualitative methodology to gain insight into the how and the why of close friendships. How do adolescents experience trust and intimacy in their friendships? Why are these relational experiences critical for emotional adjustment? And how does the social and cultural context shape the ways in which adolescents experience their close friendships? The studies reveal the ways in which adolescents from diverse cultural backgrounds speak about their close friendships and the individual and contextual factors that shape and are shaped by their experiences of close friendships.
ISBN 978-07879-80573

CAD 106 *Social and Self Process Underlying Math and Science Achievement*
Heather Bouchey, Cynthia Winston, Editors
In general, America's students are not faring well in science and mathematics. The chapters in this volume employ novel conceptual and empirical approaches to investigate how social and individual factors interact to effect successful math and science achievement. Each of the chapters is solidly grounded in theory and provides new insight concerning the integration of student-level and contextual influences. Inclusion of youth from diverse socioeconomic and ethnic backgrounds is a salient feature of the volume.
ISBN 978-07879-79164

CAD 105 *Human Technogenesis: Cultural Pathways Through the Information Age*
Dinesh Sharma, Editor
The technologically driven information economy is reshaping everyday human behavior and sociocultural environments. Yet our paradigms for understanding human development within a cultural framework are guided by traditional and dichotomous ideas about the social world (for example, individualism-collectivism, egocentric-sociocentric, modern-traditional, Western-Non-Western). As the impact of information technologies permeates all aspects of our lives, research in human development and psychology must face the digitally, connected social environments as its laboratory, filled with naturally occurring experiments, whether it is the speed at which we now communicate in the home or workplace, the far-reaching access children have to a wide array of information previously unavailable, or the vicarious anonymity with which we are able to participate in each other's lives through the new media tools. The chapters in this volume claim that the recent wave of innovation and adaptation to information technologies, giving rise to a new form of "human technogenesis," is fundamentally transforming our everyday interactions and potentially reconstructing the nature and process of human development. Human technogenesis is the constructive process of individual and sociocultural innovation and adaptation to the everyday interactions with information technologies, which significantly affects the developing and the developed mind.
ISBN 978-07879-77795

CAD 104 *Culture and Developing Selves: Beyond Dichotomization*
Michael F. Mascolo, Jin Li, Editors
The distinction between individualism and collectivism (I-C) has been useful in understanding differences in the world's cultures and the developing selves that they spawn. From this view, within Individualist (most North American and Western-European) cultures, individuals develop a sense of self as separate, autonomous, and independent of others. In contrast, collectivist cultures (for example, many Asian cultures) place primary value on group orientation, the goals and needs of others, and readiness to cooperate. However, despite its utility, the I-C dimension can obscure an analysis of the complexity of selves that develop in individualist and collectivist cultures. Individuality and interiority are represented in selves that develop within cultures considered collectivistic; conversely; selves in individualist cultures are defined through relations with others. The contributors to this volume examine the multiplicity of developing selfhood that exists within and between cultures. In so doing, the contributors examine the coexistence of self-cultivation and social obligation among the Chinese, the coexistence of deep spiritual interiority and social duty in urban India, changing patterns of identity in immigrant families, and how autonomy functions in the service of social relations among American adolescents. It is argued that individuality and

connectedness cannot exist independent of each other. Although there are dramatic differences in how they are constructed, individual and communal dimensions of selfhood must be represented in some form in selves that develop in all cultures.

ISBN 978-07879-76262

CAD 103 **Connections Between Theory of Mind and Sociomoral Development**
Jodie A. Baird, Bryan W. Sokol
The heightened attention to research on theory of mind is due in large part to the shared intuition that this core aspect of development must have important consequences for, and connections with, children's evolving social competence. This seems particularly true for the moral domain, where a psychological, or inward, focus is often taken to be a constitutive feature of what distinguishes moral actions from other kinds of behavior. Unfortunately, the theory-of-mind enterprise has largely failed to capitalize on this fundamental connection between mental life and morality, and, as a result, it has been effectively cut off from the study of sociomoral development. The chapters in this volume represent different, though complementary, attempts to bridge the gap that exists between these research traditions. Two central questions are addressed. First, what is the impact of children's conceptions of the mind on their moral judgements? Second, does children's mental state understanding influence the moral quality of their own behavior? In the concluding chapters, prominent scholars from both the theory-of-mind literature and the moral development domain comment on the efforts being made to link these research traditions and offer suggestions for future inquiry.

ISBN 978-07879-74404

CAD 102 **Enemies and the Darker Side of Peer Relations**
Ernest V. Hodges, Noel A. Card, Editors
The darker side of peer relations is subject that has been largely ignored by researchers. This volume begins the much-needed theoretical and empirically based explorations of the factors involved in the foremation, maintenance, and impact of enemies and other mutual antipathies. Using diverse samples, the chapter authors provide an empirically based exposition of factors relevant to the formation and maintenance of these relations, as well as their developmental impact. Both distal (for example, attachment styles with parents, community violence exposure) and proximal (for example, perceptions of enemies' behavior, social structure of the peer group) factors related to inimical relations are explored, and the developmental sequelaw (for example, affective, behavioral, interpersonal) of having enemies are examined with concurrent and longitudinal designs.

ISBN 978-07879-72721

CAD 101 **Person-Centered Approaches to Studying Development in Context**
Stephen C. Peck, Robert W. Roeser, Editors
This volume introduces readers to theoretical and methodological discussions, along with empirical illustrations, of using pattern-centered analyses in studying development in context. Pattern-centered analytic techniques refer to a family of research tools that identify patterns or profiles of variables within individuals and thereby classify individuals into homogeneous subgroups based on their similarity of profile. These techniques find their theoretical foundation in holistic, developmental systems theories in which notions of organization, process dynamics, interactions and transactions, context, and life course development are focal. The term *person-centered* is used to contrast with the traditional emphasis on variables; the term

pattern-centered is used to extend the principles of person-centered approaches to other levels of analysis (for example, social context). Contributors present the theoretical foundations of pattern-centered analytic techniques, describe specific tools that may be of use to developmentalists interested in using such techniques and provide four empirical illustrations of their use in relation to educational achievement and attainments, aggressive behavior and social popularity, and alcohol use during the childhood and adolescent periods.

ISBN 978-07879-71694

CAD 100   **Exploring Cultural Conceptions of the Transitions to Adulthood**
Jeffrey Jensen Arnett, Editor
The transition to adulthood has been studied for decades in terms of transition events such as leaving home, finishing education, and entering marriage and parenthood, but only recently have studies examined the conceptions of young people themselves on what it means to become an adult. The goal of this volume is to extend the study of conceptions of adulthood to a wider range of cultures. The chapters in this volume examine conceptions of adulthood among Israelis, Argentines, American Mormons, Germans, Canadians, and three American ethnic minority groups. There is a widespread emphasis across cultures on individualistic criteria for adulthood, but each culture has been found to emphasize culturally distinctive criteria as well. This volume represents a beginning in research on cultural conceptions of the transition to adulthood and points the way to a broad range of opportunities for future investigation.

ISBN 978-07879-69813

CAD 99   **Examining Adolescent Leisure Time Across Cultures: Developmental Opportunities and Risks**
Suman Verma, Reed W. Larson, Editors
Adolescence worldwide is a life period of role restructuring and social learning. Free-time activities provide opportunities to experiment with roles and develop new adaptive strategies and other interpersonal skills that have an impact on development, socialization, and the transition to adulthood. Leisure provides a rich context in which adolescents can gain control over their attentional processes and learn from relationships with peers, but it also has potential costs, such as involvement in deviant and risk behaviors. To gain deeper insight into the developmental opportunities and risks that adolescents experience in their free time, this volume explores adolescents' daily leisure experience across countries. Each chapter describes the sociocultural contexts in which adolescents live, along with a profile of free-time activities. Collectively, the chapters highlight the differences and similarities between cultures; how family, peers, and wider social factors influence the use of free time; which societies provide more freedom and at what costs; and how adolescents cope with restricted degrees of freedom and with what consequences on their mental health and well-being.

ISBN 978-07879-68366

NEW DIRECTIONS FOR CHILD & ADOLESCENT DEVELOPMENT

ORDER FORM SUBSCRIPTION AND SINGLE ISSUES

DISCOUNTED BACK ISSUES:

Use this form to receive 20% off all back issues of *New Directions for Child & Adolescent Development*.
All single issues priced at **$23.20** (normally $29.00)

TITLE	ISSUE NO.	ISBN
_____	_____	_____
_____	_____	_____
_____	_____	_____

Call 888-378-2537 or see mailing instructions below. When calling, mention the promotional code JB9ND
to receive your discount. For a complete list of issues, please visit www.josseybass.com/go/ndcad

SUBSCRIPTIONS: (1 YEAR, 4 ISSUES)

☐ New Order   ☐ Renewal

U.S.	☐ Individual: $85	☐ Institutional: $280
Canada/Mexico	☐ Individual: $85	☐ Institutional: $320
All Others	☐ Individual: $109	☐ Institutional: $354

Call 888-378-2537 or see mailing and pricing instructions below.
Online subscriptions are available at www.interscience.wiley.com

ORDER TOTALS:

Issue / Subscription Amount: $ _____

Shipping Amount: $ _____
(for single issues only – subscription prices include shipping)

Total Amount: $ _____

SHIPPING CHARGES:		
SURFACE	DOMESTIC	CANADIAN
First Item	$5.00	$6.00
Each Add'l Item	$3.00	$1.50

(No sales tax for U.S. subscriptions. Canadian residents, add GST for subscription orders. Individual rate subscriptions must
be paid by personal check or credit card. Individual rate subscriptions may not be resold as library copies.)

BILLING & SHIPPING INFORMATION:

☐ **PAYMENT ENCLOSED:** *(U.S. check or money order only. All payments must be in U.S. dollars.)*

☐ **CREDIT CARD:**   ☐VISA   ☐MC   ☐AMEX

Card number _____ Exp. Date_____

Card Holder Name_____ Card Issue # _____

Signature _____ Day Phone_____

☐ **BILL ME:** *(U.S. institutional orders only. Purchase order required.)*

Purchase order # _____
Federal Tax ID 13559302 • GST 89102-8052

Name_____

Address_____

Phone_____ E-mail_____

Copy or detach page and send to: **John Wiley & Sons, PTSC, 5th Floor**
989 Market Street, San Francisco, CA 94103-1741

Order Form can also be faxed to: **888-481-2665**

PROMO JB9ND

NEW DIRECTIONS FOR
CHILD AND ADOLESCENT DEVELOPMENT
IS NOW AVAILABLE ONLINE AT WILEY INTERSCIENCE

What is Wiley InterScience?

Wiley InterScience is the dynamic online content service from John Wiley & Sons delivering the full text of over 300 leading scientific, technical, medical, and professional journals, plus major reference works, the acclaimed Current Protocols laboratory manuals, and even the full text of select Wiley print books online.

What are some special features of Wiley InterScience?

Wiley Interscience Alerts is a service that delivers table of contents via e-mail for any journal available on Wiley InterScience as soon as a new issue is published online.
EarlyView is Wiley's exclusive service presenting individual articles online as soon as they are ready, even before the release of the compiled print issue. These articles are complete, peer-reviewed, and citable.
CrossRef is the innovative multi-publisher reference linking system enabling readers to move seamlessly from a reference in a journal article to the cited publication, typically located on a different server and published by a different publisher.

How can I access Wiley InterScience?

Visit http://www.interscience.wiley.com.

Guest Users can browse Wiley InterScience for unrestricted access to journal tables of contents and article abstracts, or use the powerful search engine.
Registered Users are provided with a *Personal Home Page* to store and manage customized alerts, searches, and links to favorite journals and articles. Additionally, Registered Users can view free online sample issues and preview selected material from major reference works.
Licensed Customers are entitled to access full-text journal articles in PDF, with select journals also offering full-text HTML.

How do I become an Authorized User?

Authorized Users are individuals authorized by a paying Customer to have access to the journals in Wiley InterScience. For example, a university that subscribes to Wiley journals is considered to be the Customer.
Faculty, staff, and students authorized by the university to have access to those journals in Wiley InterScience are Authorized Users. Users should contact their library for information on which Wiley journals they have access to in Wiley InterScience.

Statement of Ownership, Management, and Circulation
(All Periodicals Publications Except Requester Publications)

1. Publication Title	2. Publication Number	3. Filing Date
New Directions for Child and Adolescent Development	1 5 2 0 _ 3 2 4 7	10/1/2009

4. Issue Frequency	5. Number of Issues Published Annually	6. Annual Subscription Price
Quarterly	4	$85

7. Complete Mailing Address of Known Office of Publication (Not printer) (Street, city, county, state, and ZIP+4®)	Contact Person
Wiley Subscription Services, Inc. at Jossey-Bass, 989 Market St., San Francisco, CA 94103	Joe Schuman
	Telephone (include area code) 415-782-3232

8. Complete Mailing Address of Headquarters or General Business Office of Publisher (Not printer)

Wiley Subscription Services, Inc., 111 River Street, Hoboken, NJ 07030

9. Full Names and Complete Mailing Addresses of Publisher, Editor, and Managing Editor (Do not leave blank)

Publisher (Name and complete mailing address)

Wiley Subscription Services, Inc., A Wiley Company at San Francisco, 989 Market St., San Francisco, CA 94103-1741

Editor (Name and complete mailing address)

Co-Editor – Reed Larson, Dept. of Human & Community Devel., Univ. of Illinois, 1105 W. Nevada St., Urbana IL 61801

Managing Editor (Name and complete mailing address)

Co-Editor – Dr. Lene Arnett Jensen, Ph.D., Clark University, Dept. of Psychology, 950 Main St., Worcester, MA 01610

10. Owner (Do not leave blank. If the publication is owned by a corporation, give the name and address of the corporation immediately followed by the names and addresses of all stockholders owning or holding 1 percent or more of the total amount of stock. If not owned by a corporation, give the names and addresses of the individual owners. If owned by a partnership or other unincorporated firm, give its name and address as well as those of each individual owner. If the publication is published by a nonprofit organization, give its name and address.)

Full Name	Complete Mailing Address
(see attached list)	
Wiley Subscription Services	111 River Street, Hoboken, NJ 07030

11. Known Bondholders, Mortgagees, and Other Security Holders Owning or Holding 1 Percent or More of Total Amount of Bonds, Mortgages, or Other Securities. If none, check box → ☑ None

Full Name	Complete Mailing Address

12. Tax Status (For completion by nonprofit organizations authorized to mail at nonprofit rates) (Check one)
The purpose, function, and nonprofit status of this organization and the exempt status for federal income tax purposes:
☐ Has Not Changed During Preceding 12 Months
☐ Has Changed During Preceding 12 Months (Publisher must submit explanation of change with this statement)

13. Publication Title	14. Issue Date for Circulation Data Below
New Directions for Child and Adolescent Development	Summer 2009

15. Extent and Nature of Circulation			Average No. Copies Each Issue During Preceding 12 Months	No. Copies of Single Issue Published Nearest to Filing Date
a. Total Number of Copies (Net press run)			778	773
b. Paid Circulation (By Mail and Outside the Mail)	(1)	Mailed Outside-County Paid Subscriptions Stated on PS Form 3541 (Include paid distribution above nominal rate, advertiser's proof copies, and exchange copies)	162	160
	(2)	Mailed In-County Paid Subscriptions Stated on PS Form 3541 (Include paid distribution above nominal rate, advertiser's proof copies, and exchange copies)	0	0
	(3)	Paid Distribution Outside the Mails Including Sales Through Dealers and Carriers, Street Vendors, Counter Sales, and Other Paid Distribution Outside USPS®	0	0
	(4)	Paid Distribution by Other Classes of Mail Through the USPS (e.g. First-Class Mail®)	0	0
c. Total Paid Distribution (Sum of 15b (1), (2), (3), and (4))			162	160
d. Free or Nominal Rate Distribution (By Mail and Outside the Mail)	(1)	Free or Nominal Rate Outside-County Copies included on PS Form 3541	43	43
	(2)	Free or Nominal Rate In-County Copies included on PS Form 3541	0	0
	(3)	Free or Nominal Rate Copies Mailed at Other Classes Through the USPS (e.g. First-Class Mail)	0	0
	(4)	Free or Nominal Rate Distribution Outside the Mail (Carriers or other means)	0	0
e. Total Free or Nominal Rate Distribution (Sum of 15d (1), (2), (3) and (4))			43	43
f. Total Distribution (Sum of 15c and 15e)		▶	205	203
g. Copies not Distributed (See Instructions to Publishers #4 (page #3))		▶	573	570
h. Total (Sum of 15f and g)		▶	778	773
i. Percent Paid (15c divided by 15f times 100)		▶	79%	79%

16. Publication of Statement of Ownership

☐ If the publication is a general publication, publication of this statement is required. Will be printed in the __Winter 2009__ issue of this publication.   ☐ Publication not required.

17. Signature and Title of Editor, Publisher, Business Manager, or Owner	Date
Susan E. Lewis, VP & Publisher - Periodicals _(signature)_	10/1/2009

I certify that all information furnished on this form is true and complete. I understand that anyone who furnishes false or misleading information on this form or who omits material or information requested on the form may be subject to criminal sanctions (including fines and imprisonment) and/or civil sanctions (including civil penalties).

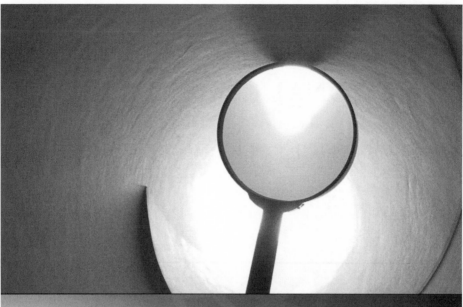